*f*P

IF ONLY WE KNEW WHAT WE KNOW

The Transfer of Internal Knowledge and Best Practice

CARLA O'DELL

C. JACKSON GRAYSON, JR.

with Nilly Essaides

THE FREE PRESS

THE FREE PRESS
A Division of Simon & Schuster Inc.
1230 Avenue of the Americas
New York, NY 10020

Designed by Carla Bolte

Manufactured in the United States of America

10 9 8 7 6 5 4

Library of Congress Cataloging-in-Publication Data
O'Dell, Carla S., date.
If only we knew what we know : the transfer of internal knowlege and best practice / Carla O' Dell, C. Jackson Grayson, Jr., with Nilly Essaides.
p. cm.
Includes bibliographical references and index.
1. Organizational learning. 2. Knowledge management.
3. Communication in organizations. 4. Benchmarking (Management).
I. Grayson, C. Jackson (Charles Jackson), date. II. Essaides, Nilly. III. Title.
HD58.82.03 1998 98-18441 CIP
658.3'124—dc21

ISBN 0–684–84474–5

To APQC's International Benchmarking Clearinghouse Members who always gave so generously of their time and best practices to us and to each other; to the pathbreaking companies and people who shared with us their knowledge, experiences, and insights; to the superb staff of APQC who share a dedication to excellence and the mission; and finally, to our families for their love and understanding.

CONTENTS

Preface *ix*

Acknowledgments *xvii*

PART ONE: A FRAMEWORK FOR INTERNAL KNOWLEDGE TRANSFER

1. Definitions of Knowledge and Knowledge Management 3
2. KM in Action—The Transfer of Best Practices 11
3. The Barriers to Internal Transfer. 16
4. A Model for Best Practice Transfer 21

PART TWO: THE THREE VALUE PROPOSITIONS

5. Find Your Value Proposition 31
6. Customer Intimacy 38
7. Product-to-Market Excellence 47
8. Achieving Operational Excellence 59

PART THREE: THE FOUR ENABLERS OF TRANSFER

9. Culture, the Unseen Hand 71
10. Using Information Technology to Support Knowledge Transfer. 85

11. Creating the Knowledge Infrastructure 107
12. Measuring the Impact of Transfer 126

PART FOUR: REPORTS FROM THE FRONT LINES: PIONEER CASE STUDIES

13. The View from the Top 141
14. Buckman Laboratories: Empowered by K'Netix® 144
15. TI's Best Practice Sharing Engine 152
16. Becoming a "Knowledge Bank" 160
17. Sequent Computer's Knowledge "Slingshot" 170

PART FIVE: THE FOUR-PHASE PROCESS: OR "WHAT DO I DO ON MONDAY MORNING?"

18. Plan, Assess, and Prepare: Phase 1 183
19. Designing the Transfer Project: Phase 2 191
20. Implementation: Phase 3 199
21. Transition and Scale-Up: Phase 4 208

PART SIX: CONCLUSION

22. Enduring Principles 223

Appendix
The Knowledge Management Assessment Tool (KMAT)©. . 227

References 231
Index 233

PREFACE

If TI only knew what TI knows.
—Jerry Junkins, ex-CEO of Texas Instruments

I wish we knew what we know at HP.
—Lew Platt, Hewlett-Packard

Arthur Clarke once observed that cave dwellers froze to death on beds of coal. Coal was right under them, but they couldn't see it, mine it, or use it. This is one clear case of what you don't know can and will hurt you. And it's happening all over again in the 1990s. Except that this time around, it's not beds of coal but beds of "knowledge"—hidden reservoirs of intelligence that exist in almost every organization, relatively untapped and unmined.

A few organizations, however, are not making this mistake. They're learning how to mine knowledge with machinery called "knowledge management" (KM). They are tapping into this hidden asset, capturing it, organizing it, transferring it, and using it to create customer value, operational excellence, and product innovation—all the while increasing profits and effectiveness.

From Amoco to Xerox, Buckman to Sequent, companies are rallying their workers around the "sharing what we know" battle cry. There already are clear signs that effective transfer of knowledge pays off—*big time*.

HOW WE CAME TO KNOW WHAT WE KNOW

The American Productivity & Quality Center (APQC) has been observing and studying the evolution of the transfer of best practices and knowledge management since they first appeared on the radar screen of American industry. The APQC is a nonprofit source for performance improvement and decision support—information and knowledge, networking, research, training, and advisory services—located in Houston, Texas. Through APQC's International Benchmarking Clearinghouse and its Institute for Education Best Practices, organizations of all sizes and industries—business, government, education, and health care—partner with APQC to discover global best practices and grow into learning organizations. We bring consertia of organizations together to find best practices, including four consortia we have formed on knowledge management and the transfer of best practices (see APQC references). It is through working with those organizations that we have discovered much of what we share in this book.

At first, the signals were but a faint flicker: Shortly after the APQC founded the International Benchmarking Clearinghouse in 1992, we began to notice that as we searched for best practices for our members, we were turning up many cases of unknown and unshared knowledge in the *very* firms doing the benchmarking. The grass was greener in their own back yard. And they did not even know it. We were puzzled. These were not your average, run-of-the-mill companies. These were winners. Pursuers of best practices. Seekers of new ideas. Some of the most intellectually curious, performance-oriented organizations in the world. Yet they did not even know about practices hidden, untouched and undocumented, inside the walls of their own organizations.

Perplexed, we asked our member companies to participate in pathbreaking research on best practices transfer. Led by Dr. Gabriel Szulanski (formerly with INSEAD and now assistant professor of management with the Wharton School of Business), this 1994 study was the first practical study of the phases and barriers to effective transfer of knowledge in organizations. (More details about Szulanski's findings can be found in Chapter 3.)

Why didn't knowledge and practices transfer?

It wasn't because people are inherently turf-protecting, knowledge-hoarding beings. Not at all! Szulanski found that the number one, biggest barrier to the transfer was *ignorance*. And ignorance on both ends of the transfer. At most companies, particularly large ones, neither the "source" nor the "recipient" knew someone else had knowledge they required or would be interested in knowledge they had. The most common response from employees was either "I didn't know that you needed this" or "I didn't know that you had it."

Once people recognized that a better practice existed, the second biggest barrier to transfer was the *absorptive capacity* of the recipient: Even if a manager knew about the better practice, he or she might have neither the resources (time or money) nor enough practical detail to implement it.

The third barrier to transfer was the *lack of a relationship* between the source and the recipient of knowledge; that is, the absence of a personal tie, credible and strong enough to justify listening to or helping each other, stood in the way of transfer.

Finally—and here's the real shocker—Szulanski found that even in the best of firms, in-house best practices took an average of *twenty-seven months* to wind their way from one part of the organization to another. Over two years' lag time, in an era when new companies are launched every nanosecond and information rushes through network cyberveins at lightning speed. Nothing we have learned since then has affected our world view as much as this one bit of information.

We have shared Szulanski's insights widely with our five-hundred-plus APQC International Benchmarking Clearinghouse member organizations. They have led many to freshly examine the role and methodology of knowledge transfer in creating value in their own organizations. We began to see more and more little flickers of light on our radar screen.

These organizations didn't know what they knew. We began to study and work with organizations who *did* know, and many others determined to emulate them.

This book is about those who seek excellence in their own back yards. It is the product of three years of listening, questioning, observing, cooperating, facilitating, and synthesizing the experiences of over seventy companies that have embraced knowledge transfer as a strategic thrust for the twenty-first century. It is the latest effort in a long quest to understand how organizations can derive value from the knowledge that lies throughout their operations.

WHAT YOU DON'T KNOW WILL COST YOU—OR RUIN YOU

How can you succeed in the knowledge era without knowing what you know?

You can't.

Only those organizations that methodically, passionately, and proactively find out and transfer what they know, and use it to increase efficiency, sharpen their product-development edge, and get closer to their customers, will not only survive, but excel.

The book is organized around the following main messages:

1. Knowing how to transfer and leverage knowledge and best practices will make you money.
2. To turn knowledge into profit, you must focus your transfer efforts on one (or more) of three value propositions: (a) improving customer intimacy and customer-related processes and practices, (b) honing product-to-market excellence, and/or (c) achieving operational excellence.
3. Finally, to ensure grand designs turn into real-life improvements, you need a process model and road map for making KM and best-practice transfer work. Change without a recipe is a recipe for chaos. The transfer model must describe not only the steps in the process, but also the *enabling context* that is critical to its success: organizational infrastructure, culture, information technology, and measurement. These "enablers" will either help or hinder your progress.

WHY READ THIS BOOK?

This is not the first book about managing of transferring knowledge and it is certainly not the last book about knowledge management (KM). There are many excellent books about knowledge management per se (Davenport and Prusak, 1998; Edvinsson and Malone, 1997; Stewart, 1997; Svieby, 1997), but we think our book is unique.

Here's why:

First, this book is not only about why knowledge matters. We all know it does. It's a book about how to improve the performance of your organization; it's about how to generate profits using *existing methodologies* and *in-house know-how*. We don't advocate that you go out and buy expensive new systems. We don't necessarily think you must hire more consultants. What we do strongly advocate is the use of a specific KM vehicle that we know, for a fact, works: the identification and transfer of best practices. More than 80 percent of KM practitioners in our studies rely on the internal *transfer of best practices* to grow their collective IQ. And with stunning results.

Second, this book is not based on theories or speculation. It is anchored in successes, mistakes, and real-life case studies. It is not a spiritual guide or a technology manual. The experiences, thoughts, insights, and conclusions herein are based on surveys, site visits, and design work with over seventy organizations of all shapes and sizes. The APQC has conducted four major Consortium Benchmarking Studies on knowledge management with results of unprecedented scope and depth (APQC, 1996, 1997, 1998). The behind-the-scenes look they offer, at the *why and how* of KM and best practice transfer, is a veritable treasure chest of knowledge. And we want to share it with you.

This book is primarily about *internal transfer of best practices* in organizations. That is, the transfer of best practices from one part of an organization to another part—or parts—in order to increase profitability or effectiveness. We know it works. We have evidence that it works. And we will share this with you throughout the book with numerous case study examples from leading organizations, both profit-making and nonprofit.

Finally, it is also a book about the transfer of *knowledge*, specifically, the effective management of knowledge inside an organization. Transferring best practices within an organization is much more effective when it is part of an overall environment that values the sharing of knowledge.

This book will focus largely on "internal benchmarking"—looking inside your own organization—and transferring best practices. (Of course, there is also great value in looking *outside* your organization—

"external benchmarking.") We find that benchmarking and knowledge management benefit from each other the way a desktop PC becomes more powerful once equipped with a browser and connected to an intranet. Each is a useful tool itself. Together, what you create locally on your PC can be shared widely, and what others have learned is accessible to you through the intranet.

Benchmarking is the process of finding and adapting best practices. Once you have done so, a knowledge management system helps to spread the useful practices around the organization. Otherwise, even the best practices will only have local benefit, or spread leisurely or by luck. (Europe certainly would have benefited from a better knowledge management system after Marco Polo benchmarked the Chinese.)

To benchmark as a verb means to systematically identify and learn from best practices, internal or external, in order to improve your own performance. The noun benchmark is a measure of performance. Benchmarks tell you how good others are. Benchmarking tells you how to get there. You need both. Done right, benchmarking is less a study than a contact sport; a method of learning how to learn, and a key component of knowledge creation, adaptation, and implementation.

Since the early 1990s we've seen dramatic acceptance of benchmarking as a legitimate way to speed improvement and change. Xerox, Chevron, Texas Instruments, Kodak, IBM, Citibank, GE, Amgen, GTE, AT&T, and the U.S. Postal Service are emphatic about the need to overcome the Not-Invented-Here syndrome and adopt best practices.

As evidence of the exploding activity in benchmarking, APQC's International Benchmarking Clearinghouse has over five hundred member organizations—a blue-ribbon group from business, government, health care, and education—that are constantly sharing knowledge with one another and seeking best practices in other sectors and countries. Many of our members are from Canada, Asia, Australia, South America, and Europe. Other benchmarking centers are being created, such as the Asian Benchmarking Center, the Commonwealth Benchmarking Club, and an Indonesian Benchmarking Clearinghouse. APQC has taught benchmarking in over thirty countries. APQC is partnering with the European Foundation for Quality Management on a number of benchmarking studies.

Successful benchmarking has actually led managers to see how powerful and profitable managing knowledge can be. A word of caution: sharing only *internal* knowledge and practices can lead to myopia and the self-delusion that you are best. *External* benchmarking scours across sectors and industries for excellence, causing goals to be set much higher. Gains of as much as 30 to 50 percent are achieved.

Benchmarking can also help feed a knowledge management system's voracious appetite for useful content. People want to know: "Who has looked at this issue before?" "Has anyone benchmarked this process?" "What did they learn?" Texas Instruments and Chevron have extremely active repositories on-line that track past, current, and planned benchmarking studies, provide a quick summary of the status or results, and say whom to contact for more information.

Finally, when their forces are combined, benchmarking and knowledge management accelerate change: As Bob George of DuPont said, "Benchmarking is a change management process and the one we use at DuPont." One of the reasons it works so well is that skeptics get proof that best practices can work—seeing is believing. One manager of Xerox said: "The only way to convince most managers of a new way was to allow them to witness it with their own eyes. Talking to them didn't do the trick."

Benchmarking and knowledge management are like love and marriage. You can have one without the other. But it's far better if you have both.

Finally, as you read this book, there will be times you will be skeptical. That's okay. So were we initially. We too have seen every fad in the last twenty years. We do not think knowledge management and best practices transfer are a fad. They do need heightened emphasis now, but in a few years they will be standard operating procedures for successful firms, like just-in-time, cycle time reduction, and total quality.

Be critical, but don't be cynical. "It's early days for KM," says our friend Tom Davenport, professor of management information systems at Boston University. We know that identifying, managing, and transferring knowledge and best practices has worked for some companies, sometimes saving or earning them literally billions. What we've seen is impressive. It's important. If we wait to know all there is to know, we may well be too late.

ACKNOWLEDGMENTS

Over a year ago, we decided to write this book to find out what we know about the transfer of internal knowledge and best practices, for as someone said, "I don't know what I think until I write." But we also said, "If only we knew what *they* knew," meaning the leading organizations who are experimenting, inventing, learning, and changing in this rapidly expanding work of transfer of internal knowledge and best practices. To create this book, we have learned from literally hundreds of organizations, whether they shared experiences or questions. Over twenty companies you will read about let us visit them, spend time at their sites, and publish their stories.

For their help on the detailed case studies in Part Four, we would especially like to thank Robert Buckman from Buckman Laboratories, Melissie Rumizen, formerly with the National Security Agency and now with Buckman; Bill Spencer with NSA, Dave Ledet, Bill Lowrie, and Don Tornberg of Amoco; John Davis of AMP; Bob Hiebeler of Arthur Andersen; Ken Derr, Mike Callaghan, Greta Lydecker, Jim O'Brient, and Jim Tighe of Chevron; Marc Demarest and Roger Swanson of Sequent; Tom Engibous, Cindy Johnson, and Bill Baker of Texas Instruments; Steve Denning of the World Bank; and Mary Halaszyn and Susan Sellier of APQC for their attention to infinite detail and coordination, good judgment, and good humor. The APQC teams who conduct our KM and transfer projects are the real creators of knowledge we share here. Many thanks to Peggy Odem, Stephanie Carlin, Linda Muchisky, and Cindy Hubert for leading the way.

Part One

A FRAMEWORK FOR INTERNAL KNOWLEDGE TRANSFER

Part One lays the foundation for the rest of the book. In Chapter 1 we provide our working definitions of knowledge and knowledge management (KM). Is it a fad, soon to fade, or something real? Answer: It's for real.

In Chapter 2, we discuss "KM in Action: Transfer of Best Practices," and we give a few illustrations of transfer. More extensive examples will come later in the book after we have laid the foundation.

In Chapter 3, we go deeper into the "Barriers to Internal Transfer," for "transfer" isn't as easy as it may sound at first.

In Chapter 4, we provide an overview of the components of creating a successful transfer system: discovering your value proposition; creating the environmental enablers; and embarking on a structured process for designing the entire initiative.

Chapter 1

DEFINITIONS OF KNOWLEDGE AND KNOWLEDGE MANAGEMENT

Knowledge management is really about recognizing that regardless of what business you are in, you are competing based on the knowledge of your employees.

—*Cindy Johnson, Director of Collaboration and Knowledge Sharing at Texas Instruments*

WHAT DO WE MEAN BY "KNOWLEDGE"?

The recorded study of learning and knowledge dates back at least to Plato and Aristotle; however, its modern-day exploration is credited to thinkers like Daniel Bell (1973), Peter Drucker (1993), Alvin Toffler (1970, 1980), and the philosopher Michael Polanyi (1958, 1967). Polanyi's work served as the basis for the much-acclaimed knowledge management theories and books by the Japanese organizational learning guru, Ikujiro Nonaka (1991, 1995)—as of September 1997 appointed Xerox Chair of Knowledge at his alma mater, The Haas School of Business, the University of California at Berkeley.

Polyani and Nonaka both point out that knowledge comes in two basic varieties: *tacit* and *explicit*, also known as informal/uncodified and formal/codified. Explicit knowledge comes in the form of books and documents, white papers, databases, and policy manuals. The tacit/uncodified variety, in contrast, can be found in the heads of employees, the experience of customers, the memories of past vendors. Tacit knowledge is hard to catalogue, highly experiential, difficult to document in any detail, ephemeral and transitory. Both types of knowledge are important.

Some may argue that, in a commercial context, tacit knowledge does not qualify as "knowledge" at all. Just as value is defined by the "transfer price" in the context of seller/buyer interaction, thoughts in our heads are not "knowledge" until they enter the marketplace of ideas via discussion and interaction. "It is the intersection between tacit knowledge and explicit knowledge that creates learning," Nonaka wrote in the February 1994 issue of *Organizational Science*.

For example, a manager who has just tried out a new sales technique has "tacit" knowledge of it. If he writes it down and posts it on his company's intranet site, some of that knowledge has become captured and "explicit." Next, another sales manager reads the description and uses the technique on her next sales trip (hence turns it into "tacit" once more). Knowledge has been captured, exchanged, and created (see Steps in the Knowledge Transfer Process, below). The learning process hence involves the continuous "intersection" of these two knowledge types and a never-ending, closed-loop transformation process.

Other organizational experts, such as Leif Edvinsson of Skandia, further divide commercial knowledge into *individual*, *organizational*, and *structural* knowledge. Individual knowledge is solely in the minds of employees. Organizational knowledge is the learning that occurs on a group or division level. Structural knowledge is embedded in the "bricks" of the corporation though processes, manuals, and codes of ethics. At any one of these three "states," the knowledge can be either tacit or explicit.

Knowledge is broader than intellectual capital (IC). Whereas some writers have chosen to expand IC to include practices and processes, in its purest form, IC refers to the commercial value of trademarks, licenses, brand names, formulations, and patents. In this view, knowledge-as-intellectual-capital is an asset, almost tangible. Our use of knowledge is broader: we view knowledge as dynamic—a consequence of action and interaction of people in an organization with information and with each other.

Knowledge is bigger than information. Our organizations are awash in information, but until people use it, it isn't knowledge. While you can't have too much knowledge, you can certainly have too much information. Indeed, many organizations have already discovered that information, carried faster and in greater volumes by electronic media, leaves employees overwhelmed, not overconfident. Fumbling rather than focused. Paralyzed rather than proactive.

Hence, our simple working definition: *Knowledge is information in action.* In the organizational and commercial context of this book, knowledge is what people in an organization know about their customers, products, processes, mistakes, and successes, whether that knowledge is tacit or explicit.

Data (facts and figures, without context and interpretation), and *information* (patterns in the data), are not in themselves knowledge (actionable information). For example, when a British supermarket chain implemented a high-end customer datamining application, it began to accumulate *data* on buying behavior. It then took the data and ran correlation analyses among the seemingly unrelated points to reveal buying behavior patterns. For instance, the chain quickly found a clear correlation between the purchases of diapers and beer on Friday afternoon. It took this curious piece of *information*, and hypothesized that men, on a Friday afternoon shopping expedition, are likely to buy beer (for themselves) and a pack of diapers (as per their wives' shopping list). Armed with this *knowledge* about its customers' behavior, the store took action and reconfigured the locations of diapers and beer on its shelves.

This leads us to the next fundamental question.

WHAT IS KNOWLEDGE MANAGEMENT?

Let's start with what managing and sharing knowledge is *not*:

- Knowledge management (KM) is *not* a new religion or a spiritual calling.
- It is *not* an attempt to rally disgruntled employees around an appealing philosophical concept.
- It is *not* an existentialist search for the Truth. (Actually, it's about the entirely worldly task of making money.)
- It is *not* a science or a "discipline"—yet.
- It is *not* the latest management fad.

When explicitly managed, organizational knowledge is used to accomplish the organization's mission. Knowledge management is therefore a conscious strategy of getting the right knowledge to the right people at the right time and helping people share and put information into action in ways that strive to improve organizational performance.

Fortunately, most companies have some experience already in managing knowledge. Indeed, KM is not a radical departure or a methodology in and of itself. Rather, it is a framework, a management mind-set that includes building on past experiences (libraries, databanks, smart people) and creating new vehicles for exchanging knowledge (knowledge-enabled intranet sites, communities of practice, networks).

For most organizations, KM represents a continuation of efforts begun in other times with other names (or acronyms), all of which have likely yielded valuable learnings.

- Radical reengineering may have not delivered sustainable success, but it has "delivered" the mind-set of the process-oriented organization. Processes can be made explicit, and knowledge about how to make them work can be transferred.
- Total quality management (TQM) may have not always yielded big-time change, but it laid the foundation for a corporate-wide, systematic initiative for measurement and change and cross-functional teaming, all of which, we will argue, are critical to the successful management of knowledge

Not surprising, newly trim and lean, reengineered companies like Amoco, Chevron, and Texas Instruments have been at the forefront of the KM "[r]evolution." Companies like these have been among the first to realize that to accelerate growth—again—they must adopt new approaches that leverage their internal expertise.

This leads us to another building block in the foundation for the remainder of this book.

STEPS IN THE KNOWLEDGE TRANSFER PROCESS

Managing knowledge and transferring best practices is simple in concept, but difficult in execution. It is important to lay out the key components of this seemingly simple process (see Figure 1.1). Every knowledge management and transfer initiative we will describe had to design approaches to address all of the steps in the knowledge transfer process shown in Figure 1.1.

Most companies start their organized efforts by focusing on *creating, identifying, collecting,* and *organizing* best practices and internal knowledge, in order to understand *what* they know and *where* it is. Later on, we'll cover the difficulties in these early stages, especially when dealing with tacit knowledge and know-how.

As we stated earlier, just knowing that the practices or knowledge exists is not enough to ensure transfer or use. The process must explicitly address *sharing* and *understanding* of those practices by motivated recipients. Finally, the process involves helping the recipients *adapt* and *apply* those practices to new situations, to create new "knowledge" and put it in action. This is where the payoff really comes.

DOES MANAGING AND TRANSFERRING KNOWLEDGE REALLY WORK?

It does—big time—and for a growing number of companies, large and small, private and public, in services and in manufacturing, in high tech and in chemicals. From the National Security Agency (NSA), to

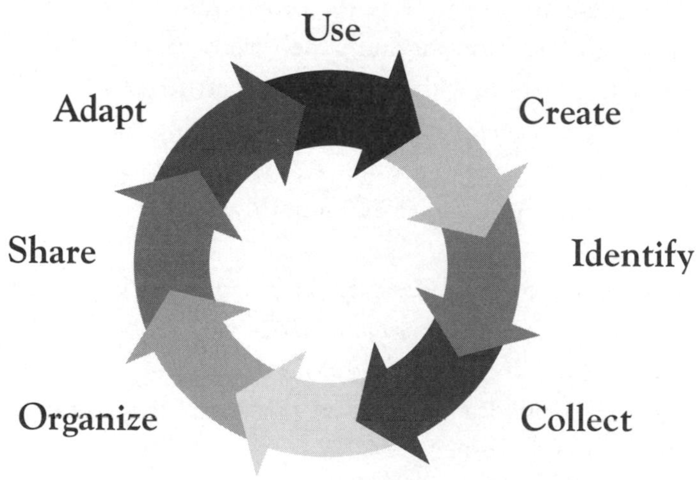

FIGURE 1.1
Steps in the Knowledge Transfer Process

Texas Instruments, from Chevron to Verifone. Megasize multinationals and small, niche players.

- At *Buckman Laboratories*, their transfer of knowledge and best practices system helped push new product-related revenues up 10 percentage points and sales of new products up about 50 percent (from 22 percent to almost 35 percent in 1996). Responding to customer inquiries about products now takes hours instead of weeks. (See case study in Chapter 14.)
- *Texas Instruments* generated $1.5 billion in annual increased fabrication capacity (in effect, a "free" plant) by comparing and transferring best practices among its existing thirteen fabrication plants. Plant managers and teams from *Texas Instruments*' Semiconductor Group, led by that group's president (now TI president and CEO) Tom Engibous, created the equivalent capacity of an additional semiconductor wafer fabrication plant, thereby avoiding a $500 million investment and providing needed capacity to customers. They called it a "free fab," and have repeated this triumph two more times, for a total of more than $1.5 billion in cost avoidance, in addition to going from last (1992) to first (1994) in on-time delivery satisfaction in customer rankings. (See case study in Part Four, Chapter 15.)
- At *Dow Chemical*, early efforts to manage intellectual capital brought an immediate kick-back in the form of $40 million in savings. Analysis of existing patents to determine which technology streams were the strongest and which were weakest allowed more effective negotiations with joint venture partners.
- At *Kaiser Permanente*, benchmarking of their internal best practices helped drastically cut the time it took to open a new Woman's Health Clinic. And it opened smoothly, with no costly start-up problems.
- At CIGNA *Property & Casualty*, knowledge-sharing efforts, combined with a reengineering campaign, lifted profits back into the black. In 1993, CIGNA lost more than a quarter of a billion dollars. By 1995, it sported a $90 million profit and has continued with healthy profits since then.
- *Skandia* has leveraged internal know-how to dramatically reduce

start-up time for new ventures to seven months, compared to an industry average of seven years.

- By comparing practices on the operation of gas compressors in fields in California, the Rockies, and offshore Louisiana, a *Chevron* team learned that they could save at least $20 million a year just by adopting practices already being used in their best-managed fields.
- *Chevron's* network of 100 people who share ideas on energy-use management has generated an initial $150 million savings in Chevron's annual power and fuel expense by sharing and implementing ideas to reduce company-wide energy costs. By 1996, Chevron could credit this best-practice transfer team with generating over $650 million in savings. And they're still going.
- *At Arthur Andersen*, a Global Best Practice Knowledge base has improved the quality of services, helped lower research costs, and shortened delivery time in business consulting. (See more detail on page 42.)
- At *USAA*, knowledge management increased the proportion of business conducted over the phone with members from 30 percent to 70 percent and helped establish ten new strategic alliances.

We will get back to these examples later in the book and in greater detail. But you get the point. We certainly did. And for us, it was a point of no return. There was no way we could ignore this outpouring of experience, interest, and practice. *We knew just how much there was to know*. And we set about to find out as much as we could.

MORE THAN JUST A FAD

Is KM another management fad? We don't think so, for four reasons:

1. It is built on the never-obsolete power of learning. As David Garvin of Harvard Business School asks, "How can an organization improve without learning something new?"
2. While there are plenty of people who treat knowledge management as a religion, real knowledge management is practical and action oriented, not ideological and theoretical. If done right, it produces bottom-line results—always a sure way to guarantee sustainability.
3. Unlike other process-improvement methods, KM does not rely on technology to make processes more efficient. It relies on recognizing the knowledge resident in people's minds, using technology to facilitate its sharing, not replace its human origins.
4. Finally, KM is consistent with emerging models of organizations. Most modern business models involve people in teams coming together on a project basis, then moving on to new relationships. All these models are process oriented, not bound by functions, industries, structures. Knowledge underpins their continuous existence.

Chapter 2

KM IN ACTION—THE TRANSFER OF BEST PRACTICES

Every day that a better idea goes unused is a lost opportunity. We have to share more, and we have to share faster. I tell employees that sharing and using best practices is the single most important thing they can do.

—*Ken Derr, chairman and CEO, Chevron Corporation*

It would be naïve to believe there is *one answer* to any organizational malaise. It's a consultant's dream and every manager's secret hope. But in real life—and that's what this book is about—such a simplistic approach often fails.

As every reengineering guru will tell you, the biggest problem with many mega-transformation efforts has been the attempt to prescribe a single remedy to a host of organizational problems. No two companies are alike.

But while there is no single answer, there appears to be a growing consensus that the fastest, most effective and powerful way companies can manage knowledge assets is through the *systematic transfer of best practices*.

This evolving consensus is not a theoretical notion. Nor is it the product of brainstorming sessions in the halls of academia or the corridors of consulting practices. Rather, it is a consensus emerging from the day-to-day, nitty-gritty, practical experiences of companies that have dared to put themselves at the forefront of this new management practice.

Sharing best practices inside organizations is not confined to the private sector. The *U.S. National Security Agency*'s Office of Plans places "lessons learned" from past crises into an on-line database available to everyone in the NSA system worldwide, 24 hours per day, and kept updated within 48 hours.

WHY "BEST PRACTICE TRANSFER"?

Because it produces results.

Best practices take information/data and put them in the context of real people and real experiences within the company. We learn by doing and by watching others do. The transfer of best practices helps others in the firm learn better, faster, and more effectively.

Recall the KM success stories we listed in Chapter 1? In virtually every case the knowledge-transfer strategy used for promoting effective organizational sharing has been the systematic transfer of best practices.

The graph in Figure 2.1 details the results of our Emerging Practices in KM Consortium Benchmarking Study (APQC, 1996). The survey results corroborate the anecdotal evidence: Systematic best practice transfer is the *one* strategy pursued by *100 percent* of the organizations pursuing value-through-knowledge.

WHAT DOES "BEST PRACTICES" MEAN ANYWAY?

We know the term "best practices" is fraught with peril; it can lead to arguments about the validity of the term "best."

Labeling any practice as "best" immediately raises a hue and cry of dissenting voices in the organization. Not only is "best" a moving target in today's world, but "best" is also situation-specific. Opponents of benchmarking have long argued that no one knows what's "best," and what's optimum in one place may not be even good for another. We agree.

That is why we prefer the terms "better" or "exemplary" or "success-

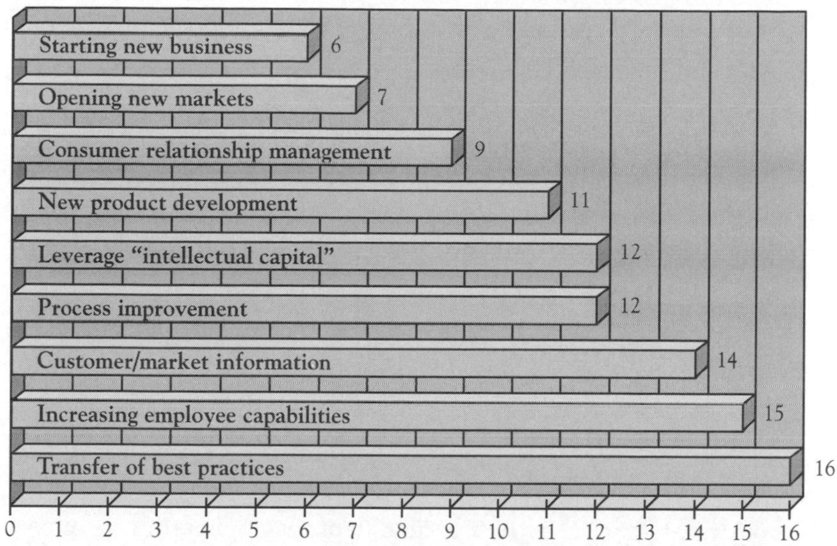

FIGURE 2.1

Objectives of Knowledge Management

fully demonstrated" to "best." But we will continue to use the term "best practices" because it has such common usage and because we do always want to strive for the best.

So our definition of best practices is "those practices that have produced outstanding results in another situation and that could be adapted for our situation."

Nonetheless, the term "best" causes problems: Internal competition and rivalry rear their heads as some units start to quibble about whether they have been measured correctly. Others rightfully raise questions about spending significant resources to transfer a practice if the potential payoff has not been demonstrated in multiple locations.

"BEST" AT CHEVRON

One way to cope with these problems is to define levels of best practice as Chevron has done. The corporation has adopted a simple definition of best practices: Any practice, knowledge, know-how, or experience that has proven to be valuable or effective within one organization that may have applicability to other organizations.

Chevron recognizes four levels of best practices in both its corporate databases and best practice teams:

1. *Good idea*—unproved, not yet substantiated by data but makes a lot of sense intuitively; could have a positive impact on business performance. Requires further review/analysis. If substantiated by data, this could be a candidate for implementation in one or more Chevron locations.
2. *Good practice*—a technique, methodology, procedure, or process that has been implemented and has improved business results for an organization (satisfying some element of customers' and key stakeholders' needs). This is substantiated by data collected at the location. A limited amount of comparative data from other organizations exists. It is a candidate for application in one or more locations within an operating company or department and possibly at other locations at Chevron.
3. *Local best practice*—a good practice that has been determined to be the best approach for all or a large part of an organization (operating company or department level), based on an analysis of process performance data. The analysis includes some review of similar practices outside of Chevron (competitive intelligence data). This practice is applicable at most or all locations within the operating company or department and may be applicable to other Chevron locations.
4. *Industry best practice*—a practice that has been determined to be the best approach for all or large parts of an organization. This is based on both internal and external benchmarking work, including the analysis of performance data. External benchmarking is not confined to the organization's industry. This process may be applicable to other Chevron locations.

For Chevron's on-line best practices sharing databases, Chevron holds contributors responsible for deciding if the practice is worth sharing with others and into which category of "best" it fits.

BEST VS. BETTER AT AMP

AMP, the world's largest manufacturer of electrical and electronic interconnection devices ($5 billion in annual revenues, and over 40,000 employees in forty countries) has taken a different tack to "labeling" practices.

For years, AMP had promoted the transfer of "best demonstrated practices." But it found that the label proved counterproductive: It gave people the impression that there was only *one best* way to do something, provoking resentment among the laggards, and fear of being accused of unjustified arrogance among the top performing units.

AMP switched to "successfully demonstrated practices" (SDPs) and added credibility to its new labeling system by establishing clear criteria for successful demonstration.

- Has the SDP resulted in measurable improvement for the organization?
- Has the SDP been recognized by internal and external experts or sources?
- Has the SDP been recognized through business assessments and audits?

As John Davis, benchmarking manager at AMP, points out, resistance to learning from others in the firm has not disappeared, but it has dramatically decreased.

These very practical definitions of "best" address one of the hurdles to transfer. In the next chapter, we address deeper issues to be overcome.

Chapter 3

THE BARRIERS TO INTERNAL TRANSFER

We are asked all the time, "If the potential payoff for internal transfer of best practices is so great, why don't all organizations do it?"

You would think better practices would spread like wildfire to the entire organization, but they don't. One Baldrige-award winner has told us: "We can have two plants right across the street from one another, and it's the damnedest thing to get them to transfer best practices."

Indeed, executives have long been frustrated by their inability to identify or transfer outstanding practices from one location or function to another. They know some facilities have superior practices and processes, and the results to prove it, yet executives continue to see operating units reinventing or ignoring solutions and repeating mistakes. It happens in business, in health care, in government, in education.

So why doesn't transfer occur?

We believe most people have a natural desire to learn, to share what they know, and to make things better. So it's not something inherently wrong with human nature that's stopping the transfer of internal best practices. Rather, this natural desire is thwarted by a variety of logistical, structural, and cultural hurdles and deterrents present in our organizations. As a result, the actual process of identifying and transferring practices is trickier and more time-consuming than most people imagine. It must involve a conscious dismantling of these organizational barriers.

HISTORICAL HURDLES TO TRANSFER

In 1994, APQC participated in research to understand what prevents the transfer of practices across a company. The study was headed by Gabriel Szulanski, assistant professor of management at Wharton. The results were startling: It revealed that a practice would linger in a company for years unrecognized and unshared. Even when it was recognized, it still took *over two years* on average before other sites began to actively try to adopt the practice, if at all (see Szulanski, 1995).

What was taking so long? Szulanski's research pinpointed four key barriers:

Reason #1: Ignorance. Those who have the "knowledge" don't realize others may find it useful. At the same time, those who could benefit from that "knowledge" have no idea someone in the company already has it.

Reason #2: No absorptive capacity. Even when employees were not ignorant of the knowledge or best practice, they lacked the money, time, and management resources to pursue and study it in enough detail to make it useful.

Reason #3: The lack of preexisting relationships. People absorb knowledge and practice from other people they know, respect, and—often—like. If two managers have no personal bond, no tie or link which preestablishes trust, they're less likely to incorporate each other's experiences into their own work.

Reason # 4: Lack of motivation. People may not perceive a clear business reason for pursuing the transfer of knowledge and best practices.

CONFRONTING SYSTEMIC BARRIERS

Whereas some of these hurdles are personal, they are by-and-large the result of a set of organizational structures, management practices, and measurement systems that *discourage*—rather than encourage—sharing. Companies that ignore these ingrained Systems (yes, systems with a big S) are naïve. To tell people to share without first addressing systemic obstacles will only lead to disappointment and failure.

Organizational personalities come in all sorts of shapes and sizes, but more often then not, they'll fall into five basic categories when it comes to knowledge transfer:

The Silo Company Inc. This multinational company has structures that clearly promote "silo" thinking and behavior on the part of managers and employees. Silos can be as small as a function or department and as large as a division or business unit. Each, however, is focused on maximizing its own accomplishments and rewards. Groups tend to hoard information to prevent others from excelling while improving their own relative performance. As a result, they substantially suboptimize the performance of the organization as a whole. As one manager said, "When it comes to bonus time, we play a zero-sum game around here. To get my share of the bonus pool, I have to take it away from someone else. Why should I share my best ideas?" Without leadership, an incentive scheme, and culture supportive of transfer, people have little incentive to overcome sharing obstacles created by departmental lines and geographic barriers.

The NIH Company Inc. At the world-famous NIH Company, the prevailing culture values personal technical expertise and knowledge creation over knowledge sharing, on either the micro (interdepartmental) or macro (intercompany) level. Otherwise known as the Not Invented Here (NIH) syndrome, this sort of attitude is rampant in engineering-based organizations as well as knowledge-based organizations, such as consulting and research firms. The reason is simple enough: For these companies, the ability to provide unique products and services is the key value proposition and business driver. The emphasis is therefore on *invention* rather than *adaptation* of existing ideas/technologies. Whether on a corporate ("we don't use what others have invented") or intracompany basis (an employee's value is determined by original thought, not necessarily clever commercialization), the resulting culture makes individuals feel "bad" if they "borrow" someone else's idea. Instead of being unwilling to share, as the Silo Company Inc.'s employees are likely to be, workers at NIH are unwilling to absorb.

The Babel Company Inc. This company suffers from an acute case of "Babelitis." Far-flung employees and sometimes even co-workers lack a set of common perspectives and terms that can serve as the basis for effective communications and transfer of knowledge. In many cases, the left hand does not fully know or understand what the right hand is doing; it may not even know there is a right hand. Different departments use different words to describe, catalogue, and record their processes and practices. Such departmental dialect impedes cross-functional discourse. There is no single, coherent vocabulary to express processes and performance. Employees may be willing to share and absorb, but without a common "book of reference" this company cannot begin to record its collective know-how and best practices. No one would understand them.

The By-The-Book Company Inc. The By-The-Book Company is not averse to sharing. In fact, however, it considers documented knowledge the end-all and be-all of knowledge transfer. By-The-Book exhibits a serious tendency to rely solely on transmitting "explicit" rather than "tacit" knowledge. It builds elaborate databases and implements distributed computing platforms that allow one and all to record and access documented knowledge. That's valuable stuff. The problem is that most of the important information people need in order to implement a practice cannot be codified or written down. Practices have to be demonstrated and "recipients" engaged in interactive problem solving before the knowledge "sinks in." Just creating databases will not cause change to happen. It will not make people share. Polanyi (1966) and Nonaka and Takeuchi (1995) have both pointed out the importance and value of recognizing and trying to transfer tacit knowledge—the know-how, the judgment, the intuition, the little tricks that constitute the noncodifiable knowledge that may make the difference between failure and success in the transfer.

The Bolt-It-On Company. This enterprising firm believes you can add transfer and sharing responsibilities on top of everyone's regular work process and expect to get results. With lots of fanfare and high hopes, Bolt-It-On starts "sharing" programs, on-line chat groups, and the like. Then waits . . . and waits . . . and not much happens. Through our work with Bolt-It-Ons, we have found that embedding knowledge practices and the information technology to support them in everyday processes and work is key. Knowledge management works to the extent that it helps people achieve their work objectives in support of the organization's mission. Overlaying additional work on top of the old way of working will not produce new results.

All of us recognize some aspects of our own organization in one or more of these exaggerated near-caricatures. Larger companies may have a NIH Company in the United States, with a Bolt-It-On outpost in Europe.

Recognizing these structural impediments, understanding them, and changing them are perhaps the tallest hurdles faced by managers today. The hurdles are large, but they are *not* insurmountable.

If you want knowledge sharing to yield the significant benefits that it can yield, you must first adopt a strong intention and a methodical approach to the management and transfer of knowledge. To get this process rolling, we have found that you need:

1. A *compelling need to change*—something that is important to the firm
2. A *clear-eyed assessment* of the current state of knowledge and transfer relative to that problem or opportunity
3. A *detailed project design* and ongoing management involvement
4. A *good implementation plan* to provide and align supportive organizational resources and structures (no surprise here)

Specifically, our studies indicate that a growing number of companies as diverse as Chevron, Texas Instruments, Xerox, AMP, and many others are taking action. To overcome hurdles and create a successful initiative requires (1) a clear focus on the desired results, (2) an enabling environment, and (3) an explicit change process. The next chapter is an overview of how to do that.

Chapter 4

A MODEL FOR BEST PRACTICE TRANSFER

The key to making best practice transfer work is to approach this challenge like the change initiative that it is.

First, change without purpose is change without direction or results. To extract value out of knowledge, companies must clearly define their *value propositions*—what they hope to achieve through the more effective management and transfer of knowledge.

Second, to ensure knowledge is created, captured, shared, and leveraged, companies must create an environment where the *four enablers* of information technologies, culture, measurement systems, and organizational infrastructure are supportive of sharing.

And third, companies need to approach the planning, design, and implementation of a transfer system with the same structured process required by a change effort of any potentially quantum-leap scale. We lay out a four-phase process.

A MODEL FOR ACTION

In Figure 4.1, we lay out a model that will guide the rest of this book. It has three major components:

1. The three value propositions
2. The four enablers
3. The four-step change process

This model applies to knowledge and practices about customers, products, processes, mistakes, and successes. It includes not just explicit knowledge. It also applies to tacit knowledge: intuitions, judgment, and know-how. As Jerry Baker of National Semiconductor put it, "Somebody held their tongue just right as they pulled the wafers out of the oven and that's what made things work."

1. START WITH THE VALUE PROPOSITION

A map is only good if you know where you're headed. Thus, at the core of the best-practice transfer model are the organization's value propositions.

The value proposition provides its unique business rationale for embarking on a knowledge-enabled change journey. Each company will have a slightly different set of reasons for wanting to transfer knowledge and best practices. Yet, we have found that value propositions tend to fall into three basic categories:

- *Customer intimacy*
- *Product-to-market excellence*
- *Operational excellence*

If these look familiar, that's because they are. They first showed up in Treacy and Wiersema's *The Discipline of Market Leaders* (1995). We will

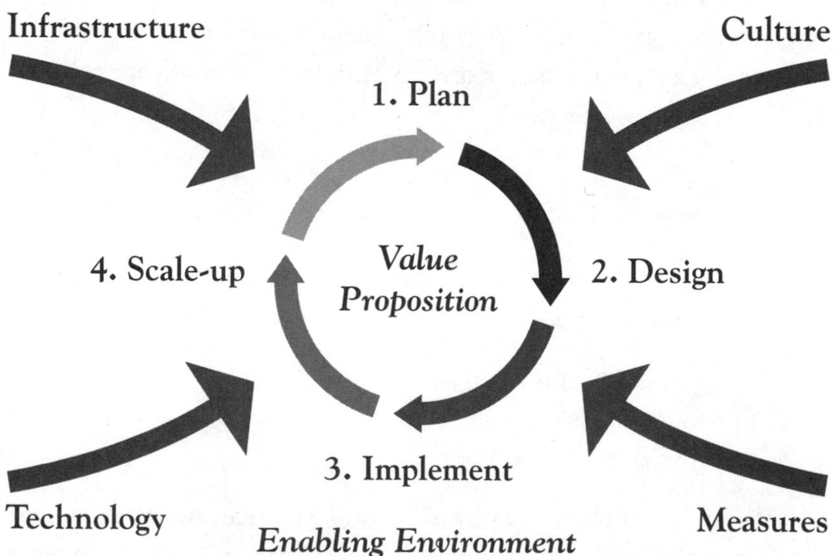

FIGURE 4.1
A Model for Best Practice Transfer

devote Part Two to an exploration of the value propositions and how transfer programs differ in focus and results depending on which one an organization selects. A short description of each follows here.

Customer Intimacy

This strategy focuses on capturing and using knowledge across the company about how to market, sell, and service customers more efficiently and effectively. By sharing knowledge about customer needs and behavior, these companies hope to sharpen their sales and marketing edge, retain more valuable clients, and provide higher-value products and services with better profit margins. Good examples in this category are consulting firms like Ernst & Young, McKinsey, Price Waterhouse, and Arthur Andersen, as well as Buckman Laboratories, USAA, and Sequent Computers. All have focused their KM efforts on arming their front-line employees—their sales force, and consultants—with the collective intelligence of the organization.

(A related, but not identical, area of KM revolves around customer datamining and help-desk technologies. But these information-technology–intense applications are examples of more statistical aspects of turning information into market knowledge, and fall outside the primary scope of this book.)

Product-to-Market Excellence

Finally, many companies are beginning to apply the principals of shared learning and knowledge management to the product development process. The idea is to use best practices in product development to accelerate time-to-market. Good examples here are Hughes Aircraft, Hoffmann-La Roche, IBM, and Skandia. Some are working hard to leverage their existing assets and patents through new product and service development.

Operational Excellence

Organizations in this category want to boost operational excellence by transferring best practices from one plant or location to receptive sites throughout the global organization. Classic examples are Texas

Instruments and Chevron. Both companies have used knowledge management principles and transfer practices to eliminate "islands" of mediocrity, create savings, and achieve process improvements and new production capacity.

2. THE FOUR ENABLERS

We strongly believe a key reason KM efforts falter is that the enablers of the KM process remain poorly understood and even more poorly managed. We will spend significant time on the enablers in Part Three, but here is an overview.

Culture

Fortunate organizations start with a culture supportive of knowledge management, one with a strong professional ethic and pride supported by well-honed skills in teaming, including cross-functional teams. It also helps to have a common improvement approach (like the Malcolm Baldrige Quality Award criteria) as a basis for thinking about work, improvement, and process. But if an organization is not so fortunate to start with a supportive culture, it must expend efforts to create such a culture, or risk failure.

How? One way is by providing true leadership. Leadership (read "senior management") support is usually gained not by proposals, arguments, or reports, but by financial and compelling competitive needs, such as "If we *don't* do it, we'll lose market share." Only a minority of firms we know of use formal financial rewards as incentives for sharing behavior. Some do embed knowledge development and transfer in their professional and career development systems. Price Waterhouse is a good example. In the past, promotions were based on seniority and tenure, which did not encourage knowledge sharing. Now, Price Waterhouse has included knowledge sharing in its performance appraisal system. Consultants must be able to produce "evidence" of actual sharing such as tutoring/training, development of methodology, publishing and presenting on topics, coaching and mentoring.

Technology

The explosive growth and ready adoption of Internet and intranet technologies has been an enormous catalyst for knowledge sharing. The key is to understand the limitations as well as the power of technology. It makes connection possible, but does not make it happen. As one manager put it, "If you wire it, they won't necessarily come."

Infrastructure

Leadership, a healthy culture, and basic information technology are necessary but not sufficient. To work, KM must be institutionalized into the organization through the creation of new support systems, other than information technology with new job responsibilities, new teams, and new formalized networking.

Robert Buckman, chairman of Buckman Laboratories International, a specialty chemicals company headquartered in Memphis, Tennessee, spent years preaching to his employees the value of sharing information about customers. They bought the message, but the payoff didn't happen until Buckman created a systematic approach for sharing know-how in 1992. The company's knowledge-sharing infrastructure uses "section leaders" as KM champions throughout the enterprise, encouraging sales people in eighty countries to transfer knowledge to the company's R&D labs about customer requirements, and to help each solve customer problems and make sales. In just five years, sales of new products have risen from about 22 percent to almost 40 percent.

Measurement

While this is the least developed aspect of knowledge management, we believe it is important to measure the projects and business processes that are being improved through knowledge management tools, and let the users evaluate the contribution. Probably the organization that has done the most in measuring work is Skandia Insurance of Sweden, where Leif Edvinsson has been able to create knowledge measures that appear on Skandia's balance sheet.

Understanding how each enabler affects the process of best practice transfer is the first challenge. Next, you will have to ensure all four are managed in harmony. If the technology allows sharing, but the culture says "keep what you know to yourself," transfer won't happen. If there are no designated knowledge champions and facilitators, even a company with a pro-sharing culture may not succeed. If there is no process for designing and managing change, good intentions will flounder.

3. THE FOUR-PHASE CHANGE PROCESS

A change initiative requires a map to guide the company's transition from the current state where knowledge is managed haphazardly, undeliberately—if at all. There may be some attempts at the grass-roots level, or none at all. The desired state is an organization that has embraced internal transfer of knowledge as a core process designed to deliver dramatic and sustainable improvement in performance.

But how do you get from "as-is" to the new and improved version? What do you do first? What do you need to consider? We will talk more about specific choices and courses of action companies might follow in Part Five, and offer tools to help you make your own decisions about what's likely to work best for you. But no matter what your specific circumstances, your change process would likely follow the following four phases. (See Figure 4.1.)

1. Plan
2. Design
3. Implement
4. Scale up

Planning involves self-assessment (Where are we today?) and a list of clearly defined value propositions (What do we want to become?). A comprehensive *design* phase involves outlining the roles and functions of people and technologies, as well as any necessary overlay to the organizational structure and performance measures. *Implementation* normally involves a pilot program (that is, a *proof-of-concept*) that will test new ideas and yield lessons in what works and what doesn't. Just as critical, the implementation stage is likely to provide much-needed success stories to drum up organization-wide enthusiasm. The next phase is *scaling up* the pilot to an enterprise-wide process to capture the full benefits of effective transfer.

SUMMARY TO PART ONE

The internal transfer of knowledge is about finding out what you know, and using it to improve performance. It is about leveraging the value of knowledge you've already got. Whereas different companies adopt different approaches to finding and sharing internal know-how, they all seem to pursue one single strategy with great vigor: the transfer of internal best practices.

Why? The reason is simple: Best practices encapsulate knowledge inside a caplet of action/experiences. Knowledge in action is a lot easier to digest and a lot easier to implement. We can clearly see it works. We can even talk to the people who made it work. Indeed, increasing numbers of companies have come to believe that the transfer of internal best practices is the fastest and most effective way to achieve improvements.

Sure, companies have embarked on change efforts before. This one is different. It's different because the improvement work is anchored in real-life practical knowledge—the know-how and intelligence other people within your own company have developed and used. It has worked for others. It can work for you.

The key for making this work is threefold:

1. You've got to have a clearly defined purpose: *the value proposition*.
2. You've got to understand and leverage various organizational *enablers*, from infrastructure to technology, from measurement to culture.
3. You've got to have an organized way for achieving it: *the four-phase process*.

The remainder of this book is about these three components and the companies that illustrate their effective use.

Part Two

THE THREE VALUE PROPOSITIONS

Companies must transfer knowledge and best practices to create value, *and value is created by translating knowledge into action. But exactly what "value" are we talking about? Higher stock value? Higher dollar sales? Fatter profit margins?*

The following section presents examples of how companies harness their know-how and best practice transfer efforts to achieve one of three specific value propositions: customer intimacy, product-to-market excellence, or operational excellence.

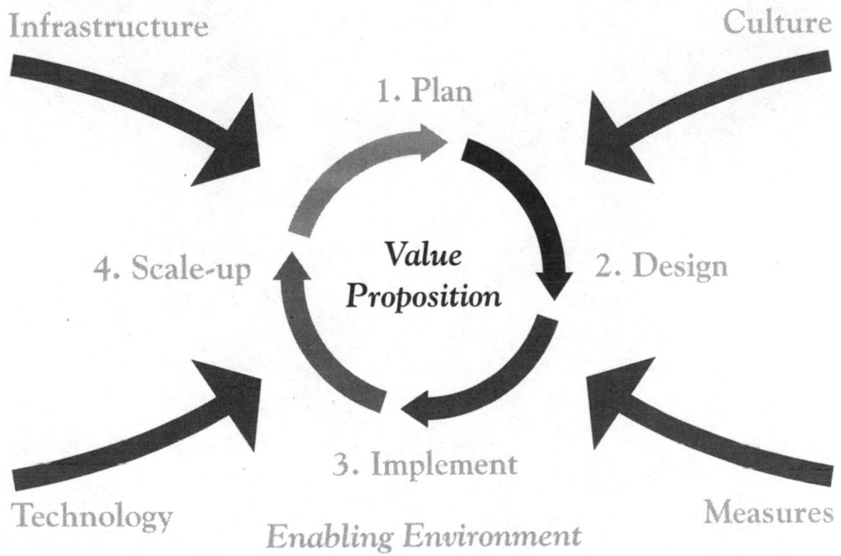

A Model for Best Practice Transfer

Chapter 5

FIND YOUR VALUE PROPOSITION

Knowledge creates value when it is put into action. But not just *any* knowledge or *any* action. An enthusiastic exhortation of "Let's all share!" is likely to go unheeded—if you are lucky. If you aren't, dozens of erratic—albeit well-intentioned—attempts at transfer will be launched, only to quickly fall back to earth with little to show for the effort.

To translate knowledge into value, companies need *focus*. They need to take a hard look at the set of challenges and opportunities that drive their particular business. Next, they must determine the areas in which sharing of knowledge and best practices can help improve performance.

The first step in a firm's pursuit of knowledge and best practice transfer is identifying its own value proposition: What is the strategic problem or process that could be improved if knowledge about best practices were better shared and transferred in *your* organization? Exhortations to "share" are just so much hype without a business problem that people really want to solve. The key to effective management of knowledge is to create processes that will put that knowledge into action.

DIFFERENT STROKES FOR DIFFERENT FOLKS

A *value proposition* is the logical link between action and payoff: *If we do A, then B will happen, and the return on B is higher than either the cost of A or the potential risk of not making B happen*. The value proposition is the business case for action (and investment).

Each company has a different set of factors that drive or impede its performance. For banks and utilities, caught in the throes of deregulation, reinvigorating *customer intimacy* is a key driver of value.

Some high-tech firms, in contrast, compete more on the speed of product innovation than on whether or not they remember their customers' birthdays. For them, best practice in *product development* is an important driver of success.

Finally, capital-intensive organizations such as chemical firms often find that *operational excellence* is a "make or break" proposition. If their plants churn out less product at higher cost, they have no hope of competing effectively.

For any firm, however, getting value from transfer of knowledge and best practices starts with focusing efforts on that firm's value proposition. Ask yourself this: Do you want to compete on the basis of customer knowledge and service, product development and time-to-market; or low-cost, high-quality operational efficiency? All? Two of three?

FOCUS, FOCUS, FOCUS . . .

Why is it so critical that companies define their value proposition and focus their efforts accordingly?

Focus ensures valuable resources are applied to high-payoff areas. There are only so many resources to spend on managing knowledge. By figuring out what counts—first—companies have a better chance at reaping big-time results, boosting not only the bottom line but also the credibility of the transfer effort.

For example, before Sequent Computer Systems, Inc. launched a company-wide best practice and knowledge sharing initiative, it identified three business features that affect profitability:

- knowledge-intensive pressure points in its value chain
- a detailed model of cycle time and flow in its channel operations
- a good handle on project costs

Sequent then focused its transfer initiatives on points in the value chain that (a) reduce project cycle time, (b) decrease costs, (c) increase volume (of customers, projects, and therefore revenue), or (d) manage risks associated with operations.

Focus helps guarantee transfer of the "right" knowledge. It helps people determine what knowledge should be captured and transferred and allows people to see a clear reason for this KM and transfer activity.

Finally, focus gets management's attention—and funding. Senior management is bombarded daily with requests to support some program that is going to "transform the company." Most have seen enough fads come and go; they are no longer swayed by glossy proposals or snazzy reports. What does catch management's attention is demonstrated results (a.k.a. financial); successes within their organization or at other firms which they respect; or a compelling competitive need ("if we don't do it, we'll lose market share").

One certain way to get executives involved is to ask them to define what knowledge they think is valuable and where they think the organization is missing the boat. At Sequent (Sequent Corporate Electronic Library—see case study in Chapter 17), top executives were asked to draw up a map of the revenue "value chain," the key processes that made Sequent money, and then identify gaps where more and better knowledge could make a real difference. The company ended up focusing on its sales and marketing function.

The principles of KM and transfer may be similar across the board, but their application differs for each of the three value propositions. It differs both in the "types" of knowledge that will be captured (know-what, know-why, know-how, know-who), and in the way transferred practices will be used at the receiving end. (More on the particulars of each value proposition in the following chapters in this section.)

WHICH VALUE PROPOSITION IS BEST FOR ME?

The simplest way to choose an area of focus is to look for the *highest pain* or the *highest gain*. This is the classic methodology for targeting improvement work and investment: Where are the highest costs? Greatest revenue potential? Biggest competitive threat? Find those, and focus your efforts there for the biggest payoff.

If *you* are a senior manager (i.e., you control the purse strings), then we suggest you take a hard line and insist on a business case for profitable results (even if it costs to get one) before you invest in any transfer initiative. Perform internal and external benchmarking to arrive at an estimate of what the new initiatives may yield in terms of measurable results and what it would cost to close the gap between your results and the benchmark level. (See Part Five.)

Ultimately, companies should align their transfer work with their strategy for competitive advantage. One should feed the other. When Sequent figured out that its clients value its sales force's knowledge, it made sure knowledge and best practices could flow quickly to the front lines. At Texas Instruments, competition and an expensive production base forced an initial focus on operational excellence.

In their study of over forty organizations (Treacy and Wiersema, 1993), Michael Treacy and Wiersema advanced a three-pronged value discipline theory that has since become the basis for many a book and reengineering methodology.

Leading firms, Treacy and Wiersema said, have become so "by narrowing their business focus, not broadening it. They have focused on delivering superior customer value in line with one of three value disciplines—operational excellence, customer intimacy, or product leadership."

Behind the push for a more focused approach to excellence has been a shift in customers' perception of "what counts." In the past, customers judged value on the basis of price, quality, or a combination thereof. These days, value is a much broader term, encompassing ease of purchase, postsale support, dependability, and more.

For example, firms with customers that care more about support than cost can choose *customer intimacy* as their route to greatness (an example is Home Depot). Companies whose customers care more about convenience then hand-holding often pursue *operational excellence* as their road to success (for example, Dell Computers). Finally, where novelty and "first-to-market" are essential qualities, *product excellence* is the key to profitability. "Companies that push the boundaries of one value discipline while meeting industry standards in the other two gain such a lead that competitors find it hard to catch up," wrote Treacy and colleagues.

THE FOCUS CAN CHANGE OVER TIME

To say you've got to have focus for your KM efforts does not mean you pick one value proposition and stick to it no matter what. Business changes. The environment changes. Companies grow and shrink, shed operations and acquire new ones. Markets rise and fall. Flexibility is key to success in KM as in other areas of business. You certainly need a focus, but that focus may well change with time and events.

Consider the case of Texas Instruments. When TI first began to target its best practice transfer efforts, it chose to focus on improving operational excellence. But as its operations began to near world-class levels and with its market increasingly focused on new technologies, the giant multinational nimbly shifted its KM gears to a product-technology focus. Cindy Johnson, of TI's Office of Best Practices, has identified how this transition has occurred. (See TI's Value Proposition.)

KNOWLEDGE, THE NEW FRONTIER

"Know thy customer, then know thyself" was the central message in Treacy and Wiersema's article. Even in 1993 (the pre-KM era, that is), they recognized that those companies that manage to excel *not only redesign processes* but also place an emphasis on the institutionalized and *active sharing of knowledge* across functional silos.

In all of their examples, from GE's operational savvy to Dell's delivery wits, the basis for leapfrogging competition had been the *sharing* of customer, operational, and product information.

- When Kraft decided to make customers it primary focus, it empowered its sales people by giving them detailed customer and product knowledge and allowing them to make executive decisions at the local-store level.
- To launch its successful disposable contact-lens business, Johnson & Johnson relied on a call from a J&J executive in Denmark who shared knowledge of a new practice in that market. J&J captured a big chunk of the U.S. market before any of its competitors could get their act together.

But while well-managed organizations have realized the need to share "know-how" before, the mere exchange of raw data and information

TI'S VALUE PROPOSITION

On Identifying "What Counts." **According to Cindy Johnson, "The key message is the focus message. You've got to look at your business. You can't take KM and just say 'We are to become a knowledge-creating company.' Before you do anything else, you have got to find the key leverage points: Operational expense? Customer intimacy? Product excellence?"**

On Changing with the Times. **"For TI," continues Johnson, "coming off some difficult years in the early nineties, reducing operational expenses was the big-bang win. But it is already changing, to a very product-technology focus. We are now applying transfer concepts to innovation and how to launch new business and new product lines more quickly. In 1997 and 1998, the focus is on the product. Prior to this, it was operations. We could not have not have addressed all of those issues at the same time with any success."**

On Getting Started. **"If you are looking at a knowledge system, look at where it's going to bring you the returns," says Johnson. She has used the following checklist:**

- **Identify the value proposition.**
- **Understand your processes.**
- **Empower your people through teams and standardized technologies.**

"Once that's done, move forward with a people-based solution that's supported from the outset with technology to promote dialogue and cataloguing of know-how."

are no longer sufficient. To compete today and into the future, companies must up the ante of their collective intelligence; hence databases must be interpreted and the interpretation (sense making) shared broadly and effectively enterprise-wide; successful practices and processes have to transfer quickly, to help launch new businesses and new products faster—and more effectively—than the competition. High-value know-how is fast becoming the fuel that feeds the search for excellence.

In the past, inefficient processes and uninformed people made it impossible to be good at more than one area. There were not enough resources to leverage existing knowledge across departments and business units. With new technologies and new understanding of how best practices transfer, these barriers to excellence can be removed to allow companies to respond to their customer demands in ways that would not have been imaginable only five years ago.

WHO FOCUSES ON WHAT?

A snapshot of some KM pioneers' early choices of value propositions. PF = Primary Focus; SF= Secondary Focus

ORGANIZATION	*Customer Intimacy*	*Product-to-Market*	*Operational Excellence*
Amoco			PF
Arthur Andersen	PF		SF
BP			PF
Buckman Labs	PF	SF	
Chevron			PF
Cigna			PF
Dow Chemical		PF	
Hewlett-Packard		SF	PF
Hoffmann-La Roche			PF
Hughes S&C		PF	SF
IBM		PF	
Kaiser Permanente			PF
NSA		PF	
Price Waterhouse		PF	
Sequent	PF	SF	
Skandia			PF
TI	SF		PF
USAA	PF	SF	
World Bank		PF	

Chapter 6

CUSTOMER INTIMACY

This [KM] system is dedicated to the front line; it is dedicated to addressing opportunities with customers.

—Bob Buckman, president, chairman, and CEO of Bulab Holdings, Inc.

> **VALUE PROPOSITION #1**
> Increase revenue, reduce cost of selling, and increase customer satisfaction and retention.
>
> This value proposition focuses on capturing knowledge about customers, developing and transferring knowledge and understanding of customers' needs, preferences, and business to increase sales, as well as bringing the knowledge of the organization to bear on customer problems.

If you don't have a customer, you don't have a reason to exist. Amazingly enough, in our fervor to improve processes, some people actually lose sight of this fundamental. As Peter Drucker pointed out, the basic purpose of an organization lies outside itself. The customer may be a consumer, a business, a taxpayer, a soldier, a manufacturer, a buyer, or a parent. Forget that and you're toast.

So value proposition number one is: *Customer, customer, customer.*

Why would you want to transfer best practices around customers?

The obvious answers are to enhance revenue, margins, and customer satisfaction and retention. Specifically, transfer of knowledge and best practices can help:

- Present a single face and corporate image to the customer, no matter how many divisions or products you have.
- Provide "one-stop-shopping" for the convenience of—in particular—business customers.
- Give service representatives the information they require to treat customers as individuals and to answer questions and solve problems more quickly, and on the first call.
- Become so intimate with your clients—and so easy to do business with—that the "cost of exit" becomes too high for your customers to consider.
- Help sales people grow more efficient and effective at selling, cross-selling, and repeat selling.

THE REENGINEERING PARADOX

At first glance, it is surprising that the arenas of sales and marketing and customer service have frequently eluded the reengineering knife of recent years, while transaction-based "back office" processes such as accounts receivable and payable have undergone major surgery. Was it because we were all so great at customer-focused processes? Not likely. Or were marketing, sales, and service "stealth" processes that flew under the reengineering radar? We don't think so.

We think it was because most senior managers feared tampering with the revenue stream, or upsetting sales people, when they could not yet offer the tools or methodologies to truly help. Sales and service are fundamentally people-based processes, hence perfect candidates for knowledge-based principles and tools. And those tools are only now beginning to emerge.

Of course, companies have been using technologies such as decision support systems to pull customer information from massive data warehouses; some have been linking computers and telephone applications at call centers. But the "information" contained in such databases is in no way "knowledge." It's raw. It's basic. It may give service reps an edge by letting them know when a customer last called and what his or her five recent purchases were. But in most cases, only top management gets to see the results of more advanced studies of trends and patterns (real knowledge), and most systems are incapable of capturing and sharing "practices," descriptions of actions, in ways that are usable by others. That sort of sharing is almost always better handled in person, in teams, and via competency groups.

A TWO-PRONGED APPROACH

Companies can take two approaches to knowledge and best practice transfer to strengthen their bond with customers. First, they can "empower" their front-line service employees with the knowledge they need to effectively handle customer inquiries, complaints, and needs. Knowledge is power. By giving it to the customer service organization, the vague term "empowerment" finally gets its meaning.

Second, they can ensure everyone throughout the organization "knows" the customer, and keeps intimacy as a top priority.

Some of the practical strategies such knowledge seekers use include:

1. Capturing and providing the most effective sales tools
2. Giving call-center and service reps rapid access to all product and price information
3. Giving all contact persons information about the customer's preferences, prior conversations, purchasing history, and the like

(*Note: Getting to know your customers also gives you the chance to know what product and service needs are emerging before your competitors do, and hence the chance to launch new products and services; more about this in the next chapter.*)

SEQUENT'S "KNOWLEDGE-INTENSIVE" SALES FORCE

At this UNIX systems integrator (see case study in Chapter 17), KM is focused on providing design, sales, and marketing teams with the practices and tools they need to create high-end customer solutions. The Sequent Corporate Electronic Library (SCEL, appropriately pronounced *sell*) allows Sequent associates to capture best practices, proposals, designs, frequently asked questions, and customer and competitor information and make them immediately accessible anywhere in the world to any other Sequent team. The vision for SCEL has been: "The one place to go to find anything you need to help you do your job more effectively."

With multimillion-dollar projects and a sophisticated customer base, Sequent knew that the know-how it brings to each integration job is its key selling point. It simply cannot afford to put forth an "uninformed" sales person.

Each and every individual representing the firm must make customers feel certain that Sequent is on top of the issues and ahead of the competition. "Our customers cannot tolerate excessive, long-cycle, or unrecoverable failures, so we have to rule out bad design options, inappropriate implementation practices, unworkable technologies, and so forth—and keep them ruled out," says Marc Demarest, the former chief knowledge officer at Sequent.

BUCKMAN'S DISPERSED PRESENCE

In 1992, $270 million Buckman Laboratories International (for case study see Chapter 14) launched a system to help sales people in eighty countries instantaneously share knowledge with everyone in the organization, including Buckman's R&D labs. The result is a better success rate for new products, and overnight advice to help far-flung sales folks solve customer problems and make new sales.

Just as important, new ideas and customer solutions get shared widely, overnight. Bob Buckman recalls a case of a Buckman associate in Singapore who posted a request for help at 12:05 P.M. Ohio time. The first response came within three hours from Memphis. Within forty-eight hours, associates from fifty-two countries responded with knowledge. Buckman got the contract, not only because of the quality of the proposal and the quick turnaround time, but because the customer was impressed. By showing the customer the alacrity of response, the associate demonstrated the power of the total organization. The customer realized that the organization was not reliant on only one person on the ground in Singapore, but that it had the full support of the global organization, literally at its finger tips.

ARTHUR ANDERSEN EMBEDS KNOWLEDGE INTO SERVICE

At Arthur Andersen, one of the world's largest multidisciplinary professional services firms, multiple knowledge bases and information sources have been integrated into a "one-stop shop" called KnowledgeSpace[SM] for the front-line professionals. The goal is to bring the full knowledge of the firm to bear on every engagement. "Our mission is to transform the capability of Arthur Andersen, and our clients, to create, share, apply, and value knowledge," says Bob Hiebeler, Managing Director of KnowledgeSpace at AA. "The word 'capability' refers to human beings. And this is what knowledge management is all about," he says.

Why manage knowledge? "For AA," says Hiebeler, "it's really for the purpose of increasing customer intimacy; 99 percent of what we sell is knowledge. Getting close to our clients means transferring knowledge very effectively and efficiently. As consultants, our value proposition to our clients equals the combination of personal and organizational knowledge." The more of the latter that is brought to bear on the customer, the greater the value. "The whole purpose of the transfer and sharing effort is hence to dramatically increase the knowledge our people can 'tap into.' When you are standing in front of the client, you have the resources of the entire firm at your fingertips. And that has impact!"

Just what's at the consultants' fingertips? Everything from best practices, relevant engagement experience, performance measures, diagnostic tools, methodologies, tools and techniques, and to presentations, a hotline list of experts to call for more information and knowledge.

THE RENAISSANCE OF RELATIONSHIP SELLING

The examples of Buckman, Arthur Andersen, and Sequent (plus the larger USAA case study on page 43) all share a basic business assumption: The better a firm knows its customer, the more it is likely to help the customer become successful by shaping products and services to fit and anticipate his or her needs. The more you can anticipate your customers' needs, the more likely they are to come back for more and more expensive offerings.

Indeed, every study that's ever been done shows that the cost of attaining new customers is many times the cost of retaining good customers. In fields as divergent as high technology and chemicals, relationship selling is making a renaissance. Not because companies have suddenly turned all warm and fuzzy, but because fierce competition and rising "customer acquisition" costs have made companies realize that keeping their best customers is their shot at decent margins and sustainable profitability.

In the past, customer intimacy typically meant a high level of segmentation in the firm's marketing: knowing which customers bought what, when, and then targeting marketing efforts accordingly. Such "know thy customer" efforts *are* critical, but no longer sufficient.

In order for customers to achieve excellence in their operations, today's market leaders must know more about what works, and what doesn't—fast and first. They have to apply intelligent solutions quickly; they have to effectively share their best know-how and practices.

USAA BRIDGES THE GAP TO CUSTOMER INTIMACY

The driving force behind knowledge management at USAA is the need to satisfy members' requests in one phone call and continue to provide them with excellent service. Every contact is a business opportunity. To support this notion, USAA has implemented a comprehensive customer feedback system that quantifies this feedback and improves overall knowledge of the customer.

USAA was founded in 1922 by twenty-five army officers to provide auto insurance for fellow officers and their families. Today, the San Antonio, Texas-based consortium offers property and casualty insurance, life insurance, banking, investment, and real estate development services to more than three million customers, including more than 95 percent of active-duty military officers.

USAA's members are located around the world and conduct their business primarily by toll-free telephone calls, fax, and mail. USAA handles approximately 400,000 voice calls per day, and 2.5 million pieces of mail monthly. The company services approximately 90 percent of its business by telephone, from multiple call centers. The remaining 10 percent is serviced by mail.

Distance Leads to Intimacy

This long-distance arrangement creates a natural emphasis on customer service. That's especially critical for USAA, which is chartered as a reciprocal inter-insurance exchange—that is, the company's members are also *its owners*.

To ensure members/owners are satisfied and telephone contact does not breed anonymity, USAA has deployed a state-of-the-art knowledge and transfer system that performs two primary functions:

- It lets every service rep know all there is to know about *a customer* or *a problem*, and provides them with the current "best practices" for addressing issues.
- It tracks customer satisfaction on an ongoing basis, reveals regional and other trends, and shares performance measures with each and every employee so that *everyone* knows "how they're doing" all the time, every time.

Keeping in Touch

Every contact is an opportunity to learn more about customer needs and expectations. A comprehensive customer feedback system called ECHO (Every Contact Has Opportunity) helps service reps store and quantify feedback and improve overall knowledge of the customer. This feedback system lets USAA maintain and increase an already high level of customer satisfaction, track market factors and organizational considerations on a daily basis, and update each customer-contact employee on any relevant items.

ECHO's purpose is to monitor, study, and respond to member comments. This real-time customer database and problem-support system helps customer-service reps bring the knowledge of USAA to every customer's call.

ECHO also captures types of inquiries and looks for trends. Reps are provided with cases showing how to diagnose and solve a customer's problem, based on prior successful examples and best practices. The technology automates some aspects of best-practice knowledge sharing.

About 1,500 customer comments are entered per week. The comments are collected and forwarded to the proper agents for action. If the action requires a change by management, a supervisor can forward the comments to a senior manager.

The powerful system also allows anyone with access to the USAA Information Management System to do a basic root-cause analysis on a transaction recorded there. "We can look at patterns to see if, for instance, members in a certain area have financial difficulties," says Tim Timmerman, executive director of member relations and feedback.

A "Hot Topics Program" asks reps to listen for—and record in a special area—comments on new products or processes. Another part of ECHO, called "Employee Feedback," allows reps to enter—anonymously if they wish—any ideas for removing barriers to productivity inside or outside the rep's area. (At last count, the average number of "can-do-better" ideas was seventy-five per week.)

"Although ECHO doesn't collect numerical data, the anecdotal information it contains has tracked uncannily close to what we know statistically about our strengths and weaknesses," says Timmerman. About 6,000 of USAA's employees currently have on-line access to ECHO; it will be available to all employees in the future.

Just making ECHO available would not have accomplished USAA's goal of creating customer intimacy were it not for the organization's unique culture. "We have some advantages other companies do not," says Ross Miles, a business analyst in strategic planning. "There's a sense of motivation and of team." Timmerman agrees: "The excitement [and] the opportunity this culture provides is that it constantly questions itself, trying to improve the way it works. The sense of dynamism that exists here is truly remarkable."

SO, HOW IS USAA DOING?

So far, very well, thank you. USAA boasts a 98 percent policy retention rate—one of the highest in its industry—and attributes a lot of it to its culture of attention to customer needs.

"USAA is one of the few companies I have ever encountered that is totally committed to customer service," says Tom W. Blackburn, national call center manager at USAA. "With great confidence, I can send you out into the hall and you can ask anybody what the most important thing they do is. They will reply, "customer service,'" says Blackburn.

The key, says Timmerman, is realizing that knowledge is the lifeline of today's organizations. "I use a biological analogy," he says. "Organizations are moving from a hierarchical, rigid environment to one in which they are almost adaptive—the way the human body is. The body of a person sitting in a meeting is making a multitude of corrections in circulation, heart rate, body temperature, and so on, to react appropriately to the messages it is getting from the environment and from its own systems. For instance, is the room hot? Is it cold? What are the others in the room saying? An organization ought to be able to process information instantly and pass it on to the areas that need it in a similar way."

Chapter 7

PRODUCT-TO-MARKET EXCELLENCE

The only legal monopoly there is, is to get to market first.
—Rosabeth Moss Kanter

VALUE PROPOSITION #2

By reducing time-to-market, and designing and commercializing new products more quickly and successfully, we will increase revenue, retain market lead, and grow our profit margins. This value proposition is focused on two transfer strategies: (1) ensuring new ideas and new design from inside and outside the organization are incorporated into product and service offering; and (2) accelerating the product development *process* by reusing lessons learned from earlier attempts.

In our earlier sections we talked about the growing importance of speed as a driver of business change. Speed means there is less time to procrastinate on new product ideas, less time to rerun experiments or try out new products before a full launch. If you don't do it, someone else will. Once they do, you may not get a second chance.

Speed also means new products become yesterday's news more rapidly, and companies cannot rest on their laurels for decades after launching a blockbuster product. If your product development pipeline is not full of new ideas/products, your company may become yesterday's news as well.

WHO'S GOT TIME TO REINVENT THE WHEEL?

No one.

Hence the growing pressure to invent more, faster and better, is driving a two-pronged knowledge management and transfer strategy.

- Companies must ensure they're getting the "right" products and services out to their customer base by ensuring ideas and practices flow throughout the organization, from customer service to R&D, and so on.
- Companies need to use knowledge to help get products developed the "right way" by reusing what other parts of the company, at other times, have learned about getting their product to market—faster, better, and with better results.

Specifically, transfer of knowledge and best practices in product development can help companies:

- Shorten the time-to-market process (by reusing old practices and designs)
- Embed the right knowledge and functionality in the product or service (by ensuring ideas and comments flow to the right place—R&D and/or marketing)
- Consequently, cut the costs associated with successful and unsuccessful products, allowing more profitable product launches per year

Some examples of know-how and practices that help firms achieve excellence in product development include:

1. Understanding of the characteristics of good and not-so-good products and designs
2. Best practices on moving through the product development process, including how to launch a new product
3. Reusable designs and research
4. Best practices from departed (disbanded) teams

5. Understanding and use of past experience with regulatory bodies (who can slow you down faster than a flat market can)

FINDING THE BEST KITCHEN

As we were writing this book in the fall of 1997, we were struck by an article in *Fortune* about McDonald's Corporation. It described the fast-food giant's fall from grace; it concluded the once-Wall Street darling was being eclipsed by arch rivals Burger King and Wendy's (pun intended.)

Why? Mostly because McDonald had been putting out product duds and embarking on disastrous marketing efforts such as the ill-fated C-55 campaign. That's a satisfying answer to some extent. But a more revealing reason for the trouble at the Big Mac maker is found behind the slew of unprofitable product launches. At root, it appears, are three separate but related factors:

- The deteriorating relationship between McDonald's and its franchise operators
- A highly centralized management apparatus
- An entrenched culture where fifteen-year veterans are still considered the new guys on the block

"In the good old days at McDonald's, most new product ideas came from the field. The Egg McMuffin, the Hot Apple Pie . . . even the Big Mac were cooked up in operator's kitchen," noted *Fortune*. "The Corporate kitchen at Oak Brook, by contrast, has popped out mainly losers, like McPizza, the McLean and the Arch Deluxe."

The diagnosis: Combined, these factors have fatally clogged up the company's information lifelines. Knowledge, best practices, and good ideas about new products no longer transfer from the front lines to headquarters. The results are not pretty.

Fortunatley, McDonald's new CEO, Jack Greenberg, has turned things around. After spending two years working a double shift as both CFO and regional manager of hundreds of McDonald's stores, Greenberg knew customers wanted a made-to-order product. He gave authority to managers in the field, and rolled out the new cooking system, "made-for-you." It has worked: McDonald's shares are up 40% in 1998. The lesson:

in markets as fickle as food tastes, listen to the customers' real product requirements and rapidly respond. The inability to transfer or act on customer knowledge can be as unappetizing as cold fries.

STRATEGY #1: GETTING THE RIGHT PRODUCT OUT

By transferring knowledge and know-how from the front-line customer service and marketing processes to the product development processes, companies can use market and customer information to help guide the development of product and services.

How do firms do this? One common approach to transferring knowledge is to bring teams together to share knowledge about products and customers, and in the process create new and better knowledge about how and what to bring to market. Another is channeling information and comments from the sales and marketing force to the people who do the design and development work. Whether by using technology or cross-functional networks, the transfer of product experience and know-how from one part of the company to the other can reduce the risk of new product development—substantially.

Introducing a "bad" product or service is a no-win situation. "Our customers cannot tolerate excessive, long-cycle, or unrecoverable failures," says Demarest, former CKO at Sequent Computers. "So we have to rule out bad design options, inappropriate implementation practices, unworkable technologies, and so forth—and keep them ruled out."

The same is true for any firm that counts high contents of expert knowledge as part of its product or service. Take consulting and publishing firms: "Knowledge is our service," says Paul Pederson, national director of change integration at Price Waterhouse. "To maintain competitiveness we have no choice but to create and leverage knowledge."

STRATEGY #2: GETTING PRODUCTS OUT THE RIGHT WAY

Companies that have experience with the development of new products *should* know what works and what doesn't. Yet, more often than not, the experience and learning of past development efforts do not make their way in an organized and deliberate fashion to current initiatives. The result is costly waste of time and resources.

The payoff to sharing here can be tremendous. Many firms have calculated just how much money is lost for each day a product is delayed. At pharmaceutical giant Hoffmann-La Roche (see more detail on page 56), it's as much as $1 million *per day!* What's the opportunity cost for your organization?

To eliminate unnecessary delays, companies can bring together people who've been through the new product development process with those who are developing the next generation, in order to (1) avoid prior mistakes, (2) build on market knowledge, and (3) cut cycle time. And if they methodically record past practices and experiences, they won't have to repeat research, trials, and errors.

HUGHES REUSES OLD DESIGNS FOR NEW PRODUCTS

El Segundo, California–based Hughes Space & Communication has over 5,000 employees and generates approximately $1.2 billion a year in sales of communications and satellites technology to private and public sector customers.

In the past, Hughes was able to produce its products in a near "craft" environment. But as the commercial market exploded and the government market shrank, Hughes found it must cut costs and create a more structured approach. Technical excellence was considered the top differentiator in communication satellites. These days, with prices falling 20 to 30 percent per year, cost and schedule (production cycle) have become bigger issues in customer eyes. Hughes has had to adjust its business to eliminate unnecessary costs but maintain its ability to innovate and design new products.

In the production of spacecraft, 50 percent of the cost is labor, and 50 percent of that is design. Hence the firm could reap big benefits if it could reduce costs by reusing designs instead of starting from scratch every time. Indeed, Hughes has calculated a potential cost reduction of $7 to $25 million per spacecraft if it were able to reuse designs, based on the assumption that labor costs would be about 90 percent less for adapting an existing design than for creating new ones.

"Knowledge reuse is a major goal," says Arian Ward at Hughes. "Our knowledge is codified mainly in the form of product designs and other technical documents. We are working to greatly increase our reuse of this knowledge."

Hughes relies on a plethora of knowledge-sharing systems to ensure nothing is invented twice. The Hughes "Knowledge Highway" combines an intranet, a database of lessons learned and best practices, and pointers to experts and "human" networks. Editorial teams analyze captured "knowledge" and best practices before storing them on shared-access databases or intranets.

TEXAS INSTRUMENTS FREES UP INVENTION RESOURCES

If you spend time and money on rediscovering the "truth" you can't spend the same resources on inventing new products and services. At Texas Instruments, which began its quest for excellence by pursuing new operational efficiencies, the new goal is to ensure that product development can proceed without delays.

"The driving force behind KM is reduction of cycle time and freeing up of resources that would otherwise be spent rediscovering knowledge that others in TI already possess," says Cindy Johnson at TI. "These resources can then be focused on achieving innovation, which TI must have to attain greatness in the twenty-first century," she says. "Knowledge is the asset we use to create the next major innovation that will provide value to TI's customers."

NSA REDUCES UNCERTAINTY IN HIGH-RISK R&D

With an enormous range of customers—and needs—the National Security Agency, a federal agency, which monitors foreign electronic communications to protect the security of the United States, must demonstrate excellence in the selection of information to which it pays attention. And turn data into knowledge and into leading-edge R&D.

To ensure it gets the best ideas, first, NSA has set aside a multimillion-dollar annual IDEA (Innovative Development and Enterprise Advancement) funding pool for high-risk R&D. Its goal is to provide a simple, fast, and streamlined process for sponsoring exploration of technical innovations with breakthrough potential, in an environment highly conducive to sharing of ideas and innovation.

Funds are available for expenses such as research and development contracts, conference fees and travel, other types of travel (data collection or field testing), technologies, books, and other items. Agency staff can be released from current duties on a full- or part-time basis to pursue their IDEAs.

The IDEA program provides a clear and uncomplicated process to quickly assemble resources and endorsements necessary to explore new ideas. IDEA creates an environment where people with new ideas and entrepreneurial inspirations can push the boundaries of technology, processes, and methods to improve products and services. IDEA is open to the entire NSA community, and in the United States to:

- Large and small businesses
- Academic and eligible nonprofit institutions
- Government agencies and research centers
- Collaborative ventures from mixed sources

The IDEA program sponsors awardees through technical mentoring contracts and technical fellowships. For fiscal year 1998, NSA allocated IDEA funds to support approximately twenty individual projects, including in-house, contracted and hybrid efforts. The program sponsors award projects for up to twelve months and $250,000.

MONSANTO REDEFINES THE COMPETITIVE EDGE

In many industries today, from pharmaceuticals to technology to chemicals, a firm's competitive edge comes from its ability to launch new products.

Says Bipin Junnarkar, director of knowledge management activities at Monsanto: "Those companies that can deal with and make sense of incomplete information faster will have a great advantage. Those who procrastinate will lose significant advantage."

For Monsanto, the driving force behind the management and transfer of knowledge has been increasing the "sense making" capabilities of its employees, particularly in light of the "information overflow" of past years.

"By managing knowledge, we were able to increase the exchange of qualitative information and to help reduce the time to bring a new product to market," says Junnarkar. "The ultimate value of the KM architecture effort is that it has allowed Monsanto to bring innovations to market quicker, improve upon the operational efficiency of Monsanto's businesses, and serve its customers better."

THE COST OF LOST INVENTIONS

Whereas most firms have neither the time nor the resources to reinvent the wheel, is there a danger that companies' growing reliance on reuse and transfer will ultimately "kill off" innovation even where they need it most? Just how many potential "innovations" could be "lost" because people take ready-made solutions based on preexisting designs?

There is no way to answer this question with anything close to statistical accuracy, but we can venture a few thoughts.

First, there's a difference between innovation and invention. Innovation, in fact, has to do with adapting existing designs in new ways. Invention means creating something from nothing. In most firms, the latter is rare and not always possible—or desirable.

Second, is it is truly efficient for every single employee to be engaged in the process of innovation? There is no question that by relying on best-practice transfer, companies ensure not everyone in the organization will be engaged in the process of dreaming up brand-new ideas. But is it really desirable for everyone everywhere to be innovative? Perhaps there are areas where innovation is not likely to yield significant advantage, and it may take up valuable time better spent otherwise. Some things really do not have to reinvented, like the wheel (yes, that tired example).

Does KM sacrifice innovation in the quest for greater reuse? In some situations, such as the development of automated problem diagnosis scripts for callcenter reps, it probably does. But if 80 percent of cases have the same answer, innovation and creative solutions are a waste of time.

In other cases, companies have to be more cautious about reusing without rethinking. The creative process does not happen in a vacuum;

rather, it is the process of taking various existing inputs, and creating something out of them that did not exist before. To get their creative juice flowing, people need to interact, learn, talk, read, examine what's been done and reexamine it. The "creation" part cannot be automated, and it certainly cannot be replicated.

IBM RENEWS THE SPIRIT OF PRODUCT INNOVATION

Holding the largest number of patents in the world, IBM is perhaps the quintessential intellectual capital enterprise. But Big Blue did not begin to manage knowledge in an organized, methodical fashion until the early 1990s, when it began a major overhaul of its operations.

"Knowledge is core to our business," asserts Kuan-Tsae Huang, a knowledge management expert with IBM Consulting. And indeed, when Big Blue decided to manage its intellectual capital assets, it quickly realized it had been doing so for years, simply in a less explicit and organized manner.

"We've had tools for conferencing and structured discussion since the eighties," says Huang. But the creation of the Intellectual Capital Management (ICM) group was an attempt to institutionalize KM and make it more formal.

WHAT HAS IBM DONE?

To get its initiative going, IBM launched a variety of efforts, including a massive Lotus Notes deployment and an ICM intranet. Lotus Notes is a windows-based collaborative application designed to facilitate group work by making e-mail, schedule-sharing, database access, and document collaboration effortless. IBM's system is organized along competencies: logical groupings of people and resources that relate to particular business areas. The competencies cut across IBM's organizational silos. Some are processes—like supply chain management. Other are topical, like network design architecture. ICM has set a process in place to identify a competency, its members and leaders, and set up structured discussion area. In mid-1997, IBM had about 6,000 employees accessing the various competency discussion groups. By

1998 the company expects to have eighty different competencies up and running.

WHAT HAS IBM LEARNED?

First, you have to show the value of your efforts. Quoting Mr. Huang: "KM has to be useful. It requires investment. There is no free lunch. And once you do [invest], you have to show the value, or in one to two years you are out of a job. It is key to show the benefit."

Second, you need to have a framework to manage it (that is, knowledge). Without a management framework, knowledge sharing will not be sustainable. You need to be able to energize the employees, creating a vision and a value system that will provide a framework. "The core is the management system," says Mr. Huang. And from the outset, that system should provide incentives (carrots) and sticks. If you make the work part of the management or certification report, they will do it.

Measuring participation is pretty easy. IBM can measure activity, submissions of documents, hits, number of IDs issued. "But activity does not satisfy management for long," Huang says. "The next question is what is the business impact? How does intellectual capital affect performance? That cannot be automated. There has to be a separate tracking mechanism for reporting how the information was used. What did you use the knowledge for? Competition? Time saving? Revenue purposes? Making the customer happy? We measure time saving, revenue increase, and customers' satisfaction quarterly."

Third, watch out for deployment of knowledge management initiatives. Deployment of any enterprise-wide KM effort is a big issue for IBM, at both the software level (having to install a homogenous platform globally) as well as a language issue (sharing knowledge across borders, in multiple languages).

HOFFMANN-LA ROCHE GETS IT RIGHT THE FIRST TIME

USING TRANSFER TO IMPROVE PRODUCT DEVELOPMENT

When somebody starts investing mega millions in knowledge management, we know they're serious. In the case of Swiss pharmaceutical giant Hoffmann-La Roche, the commitment to managing knowledge dates back to 1992 and the start of a program La Roche labeled Right the First Time.

Right the First Time centers on speeding up the drug approval process by ensuring that the documentation required by regulatory agencies covers all the right areas and leaves no room for doubt and time-consuming follow-up questions (Amidon and Skyrme, 1997). The company wanted product development teams in different parts of the organization to share experiences and best practices from previous development efforts and documentation processes in order to cut down the time it takes to prepare documents, gather relevant data, and resolve the inevitable follow-up regulatory queries.

For La Roche, the incentive to improve sharing was sizable: In its industry, the opportunity cost of delaying a drug *for one day* can be as high as $1 million!

Hence reducing time-to-market is a critical driver of success. Plus, the competitor that succeeds in gaining approval first is able to secure patents for new drugs that lock out its rivals from years of fat revenue streams. Time is of the essence.

Focusing on Documentation

To get its program going, La Roche invested in both technology systems and the creation of a full-time project management team, aided by several hundred part-time contributors. Much of the team's initial effort focused on speeding up the regulatory approval process by reviewing past applications, and ensuring that new ones incorporate the best and brightest practices.

Putting together the documents required for approval of a new drug is a daunting task, to say the least. Typical documentation can run to 200,000 printed pages. Getting the right information into the application on the first shot, and reusing existing data and research can dramatically reduce the time it takes to prepare these documents. In addition, by figuring out what research has been done already by themselves or others, the company could cut down on costly and lengthy clinical studies.

To figure out what La Roche "already knew," the Right the First Time team examined 60,000 documents from four recent drug approval processes. In particular, it looked for follow-up questions from regulators, to see what sort of information gaps these questions indicated. Analysis of existing applications showed, for example, that some regulators ask the same questions every time. Simply making sure the documents included answers to those questions on the first shot prevented follow-up queries.

- As a result of its analysis, the team was able to design logical hierarchies—decision trees—to help put the right information into the application by following simple logic: What does the customer (regulator) need to know? Does the product work? What is its safety profile?
- The team also developed knowledge maps that help users access previously written applications and research results, as well as compiling a corporate "yellow pages" which lists experts by area of specialty, and includes their CVs and a photograph.
- Finally, by encouraging teams to use prototype documents, La Roche has given its workers a tool with which to produce, early on, key data, information, and issues relating to the approval process.

Not surprisingly, management has noted a significant improvement in the quality of documentation and the speed of development. It now takes La Roche less time to write and file new-drug approval documents. In some cases, project managers report they see a direct link between Right the First Time and their ability to come in ahead of schedule by as much as one to two months! (Based on a conservative estimate of twenty work days per month, that's some $40 million right there.)

Chapter 8

ACHIEVING OPERATIONAL EXCELLENCE

We cannot tolerate having world-class performance right next to mediocre performance simply because we don't have a method to implement best practices.

—Jerry Junkins, ex-CEO of Texas Instruments

VALUE PROPOSITION #3

Boost revenue by reducing the cost of production and increasing productivity, and raise performance to new highs.

This value proposition focuses on the transfer of operational processes and know-how from top-performing business units and processes to less-well-performing businesses, ultimately improving the organization's overall performance, reducing expenses, and increasing revenues.

Our third value proposition lies in *process and operational improvements* through the transfer of best practices.

What do we mean by business processes and operations? Everything from the back office to management practices, from production to service delivery. Any firm with many sites performing similar operations has a big opportunity here. As Jerry Junkins, the late chairman of

Texas Instruments, said: "We have world-class operations side-by-side with others who just don't get it."

We already know that just because one part of the organization is performing at a better level does not mean its "best practices" will spontaneously diffuse throughout the organization. We have never seen a best practice that could be transplanted like a begonia. More like in the case of an organ transplant, the recipient rejects the donation if it isn't recognized as "self." The implications are that people have to adapt a practice to their situation; they have to transform it and add a bit of themselves to it.

DEVELOPING A STRATEGY

Companies that succeed in raising their entire operations to the next level—and reduce variation in performance levels—know that to close performance gaps they need a conscious strategy that encourages, supports, and rewards best practices and knowledge transfer.

When can transfer of best practices bring operations up to a higher level of performance, whether it be in cost, quality, or cycle time?

1. When an organization has dozens or hundreds of similar operations, such a plants, offices, and retail outlets. Think of the benefit if performing operations even came up to the median!
2. During mergers, when two organizations want to create a true synthesis by combining best practices: not just getting economies of scale, but economies of knowledge as well.
3. During strategic alliances and outsourcing partnerships, when both parties need to share best practices to collectively achieve a desired result.

These are big-ticket items. In reality, every company can benefit when one part of its operations shares what works best with another. In some cases, simply bringing everyone up to a median level yields millions in savings and benefits. And as TI's Johnson has noted, by fine-tuning operations using available practices and know-how, firms can free up resources to focus on other areas, such as new product development.

We draw no line between manufacturers and service firms here. For consulting and other knowledge-intensive service providers, the question of excellence in operations may be expressed a bit differently:

"How can we bring the knowledge of the firm to bear on any client's problem, and look really smart to them, even if we're sending out a twenty-three-year-old to do the project?" asks Bob Hiebeler, managing director of KnowledgeSpace at Arthur Andersen. By capturing the learning from prior engagements, the practices and experiences of other teams (facilities/units/plants), the best methodologies and process redesign theories, firms like Andersen attempt to bring each and every one of their "engagement teams" to world-class levels.

SKANDIA GETS NEW BUSINESS OFF THE GROUND—FASTER

When Swedish Insurance giant Skandia expanded its "points of sale" from 5,000 to 50,000 in under five years, senior management began looking for a more effective and efficient manner of transferring knowledge and increasing its use throughout its global operations.

Core to Skandia's approach has been the notion of recycling ideas and experiences on a global scale, in order to create a worldwide base of "structural" intellectual capital, while retaining local "human" capital. That means the firm, as a whole, has worked to develop a set of common practices and experiences that are homogeneous across regions and countries.

The result is a "repeatable" process that can be transferred with ease on a need basis. For instance, when Skandia decides to launch a new business, the start-up can "borrow" administrative manpower from an already established business unit in another country to get things going. By reusing existing expertise and teaching newcomers "best tricks," Skandia reduces the start-up costs and lead time while leapfrogging productivity and quality measures compared to its rivals.

As a result of these concerted efforts to share operational best practices across the company's global business units, the lead time of starting a new business has shrunk to seven months (vs. an industry standard of seven years!). "Now," says Leif Edvinsson, vice president/director, intellectual capital at Skandia, "it's possible to complete two start-ups per year instead of only one."

TEXAS INSTRUMENTS BUILDS NEW CAPACITY

In 1994, Tom Engibous, now president and CEO of TI and then president of TI's Semiconductor Group, identified a wide disparity in yields and productivity among the company's wafer fabrication sites, each of which cost between $500 million and $1 billion to build. The wafer fabs were operating with a high level of variability in cycle time and yield—some were world class while others lagged far behind. He presented his wafer fab managers with a challenge: create a "free fab"—that is, increase capacity at existing sites equivalent to a free wafer fab site by identifying and transferring best practices from the firm's thirteen factories. "We had pockets of mediocrity next door to world class simply because [one site] did not know what was happening at a wafer fab in another part of the world," says Cindy Johnson at TI.

By using geographically dispersed teams, connecting different experts together via technology and face-to-face meetings, and systematically seeking out what works best in other parts of TI, the managers lived up to the challenge. A year later, TI boasted increased capacity equal to a new fabrication site simply by squeezing out inefficiencies and sharing best practices around the world. They have now repeated the process two more times, for total savings of $1.5 billion!

WHAT WORKS BEST?

The experiences of TI, Skandia, and Chevron (see Chevron example just below) illustrate a key point: Even after years of reengineering, process redesign, and quality improvement, most companies can still achieve significantly higher levels of productivity from their *existing* operations. Not by firing more people. Not by buying more machines. Not by forcing people to stay later and work harder. The significant improvements come from allowing people to learn what works best in other areas and try it out in their own back yard. And by ensuring they have *all* the knowledge and experience they require to do their work at their best level.

DOING CHEVRON'S BEST

USING TRANSFER TO IMPROVE OPERATIONAL PERFORMANCE

Chevron used early successes in best practice sharing to build credibility and a business case for more sharing of best practices in key processes.

Once convinced, nothing is as compelling as a CEO like Ken Derr, chairman of Chevron, who says: "Every day that a better idea goes unused is a lost opportunity. We have to share more, and we have to share faster. I tell employees that sharing and using best practices is the single most important thing they can do."

Here's a challenge: How does a $42 billion organization, with 37,000 employees in over one hundred countries and multiple, independent business units, each with its own objectives, management, and financial targets share? How can you make sure an optimal level of operational excellence across regions and business units is achieved?

Indeed, merely being big does not count as much anymore in terms of competitive advantage. Information technologies and telecommunication have enabled small firms to "mimic" large-size ones without expending hefty amounts of capital. The real advantage of size is in the access it provides to knowledge. It's access smaller firms do not usually have.

"The driver for us was in acknowledging that in a large decentralized company there is abundant opportunity for learning in a lot of different places," says Mike Callaghan, formally a consultant with Chevron Quality Staff, and currently with Chevron's South America business unit . "That is our competitive advantage in being a large company. It is not, certainly in the oil business here in the United States, being large in terms of economy of scale."

Toward Operational Excellence

In the early 1990s, Chevron's top management was looking for a way to close its performance gap vis-à-vis the competition, while still mastering the knowledge and intelligence resources it knew it had in-house. Chairman Ken Derr and his key advisors began talking about best practice sharing. "They began talking about the fact that they had seen and observed great differences throughout the company [in performance]," says Callaghan.

They also realized that a lot of the knowledge they needed to bring Chevron up a notch was right inside their own organization. "They knew that we had all this good stuff inside—we didn't use the word 'knowledge,'" says Callaghan. "All this stuff is within our control. It is all under our roof. If we could just get it spread around."

The idea was simple. According to Derr: "Sharing best practices is a way of leveraging the knowledge, know-how, and experience that has been accumulated in one part of Chevron and using it elsewhere."

The goal was ambitious. Derr wanted to create a company where "best practice sharing, reporting units working together, and cross-functional teamwork are the norm." By using a combination of hard and soft approaches, all centering on the transfer of best practices and knowledge, Chevron intended to overlay its existing operations with a neural network-like structure, which allows intelligence and know-how to flow seamlessly throughout its vast and widely dispersed corporate body.

In 1992, Chevron began systematically to track implementation of process improvements and performance metrics, while building a global summary of best practices companywide. One initiative was headed by Bruce Frolich, then vice president of refining, who quickly set up thirteen teams made up of refinery managers, operating personnel, technical experts, and volunteers. Together, they set out to examine "hard processes" like crude distillation and "soft processes" such as energy conservation with the goal of finding the best ones and helping others implement them.

Chevron defines best practice as any practice that has proved to be valuable or effective within one organization and may have applicability to another. Their initial focus was on areas where improvement could yield short-term and big-time results. For energy conservation, for example, the team first looked at Chevron's biggest energy use processes, such as crude distillation.

Chevron's value proposition was simply articulated: "By transferring what works best in the various decentralized units to other units we can avoid 'reinventing the wheel' and duplicating the efforts of others. . . . If we can share best practices—well—Chevron will have a competitive advantage," says Derr.

To ground this value proposition in a business objective, Chevron set clear targets for reducing costs corporate-wide and achieving superior total shareholder return to their competitors. Chevron achieved this goal with an 18.1 percent return, the highest among their competitors.

Combining Teamwork with Databases

The results of the original thirteen teams' efforts were placed in Lotus Notes databases easily accessible to all, and categorized by issues and expertise. "The database, however," says Derr, "is merely an enabling mechanism. The key to progress will be willingness to learn from others."

The actual learning process takes place via two main "soft" mechanisms: networks and best practice teams. The networks are more general in focus, and involve ongoing topical discussions. There are networks surrounding issues such as safety, planning, refinery operations, oil-field management, and training. Some use e-mail to communicate, others use collaborative software tools, and still others rely on "old faithfuls" such as meetings and conferences.

Best practice teams are smaller in size and targeted specifically at uncovering and transferring best practices in particular areas. Chevron's U.S. refining business currently boasts thirteen such teams. Their work is credited with improving everything from catalytic cracking to plant maintenance. Teams meet three to four times per year, usually for two days, and set aside time to share ideas and lessons learned, as well as categorize knowledge into various levels of "applicability" from good ideas to best practices.

Best Practices Yield Best Performance

The impact of this comprehensive effort of ensuring that best practices permeate the entire organization has been nothing short of spectacular. One team, in just four months, was able to identify twelve steps to monitor and thus conserve the use of expensive catalytic chemicals. "Their efforts are saving the company several millions of dollars per year," says Derr.

Another team in U.S. production compared data on the operation of gas compressors in oil and gas fields in the United States and achieved savings of at least $20 million a year by simply using practices from best-managed fields elsewhere. The energy-use network, which evolved from a best-practice team on energy conservation, saved Chevron $648 million in power and fuel expenses by the end of 1996.

And that's just for starters. "In our three pilot projects in the North American production company, the variance in performance for those three processes was significant enough that we thought that by getting everyone who volunteered to participate in the pilot phase to the median level of performance would save or create value worth about $10 million per process," says Callaghan. "That's $30 million from just those three pilots. So the actual level of achievement that is possible is significant."

Making It All Work

Deciding to share and actually reaping the benefits of sharing are two different things. According to Chevron, the key to translating words into action is in a combination of factors. Top on the list is *highly visible top management support*. At Chevron, managers act as sponsors of change, set clear expectations, and lead by doing. Of course, CEO Ken Derr's total support and leadership has been instrumental in instigating a cultural shift.

Next, Chevron emphasizes that it takes no more than six to twelve months to achieve success and gain credibility. Such *front-end loading*, achieved by picking process improvements that can yield visible change within a reasonable time, is critical for building credibility. When new transfer teams are charted, an expectation is set for early results.

The use of *experts* in providing continuity and keeping the process moving, as well as ongoing involvement from *process managers* in developing and implementing the best practice solutions, ensures long-term goals that are in line with each business unit's goals. Team leaders are usually process experts.

The bottom line is that sharing requires *behavior changes at every level*. Operating supervisors have to make the time to meet and talk about change and share ideas; technical managers must be able to cede control over R&D by discussing product innovation with marketing and front-line employees. Chevron has instituted sophisticated measurement and coaching tools to help change and reward collaborative behavior, including 360° feedback systems for appraising managers and supervisors.

The result is a new way of doing work. "If they [employees] have an initial problem, their first reaction should not be to just sit down in a closed room and try and solve it themselves. The reaction should be to go and ask questions, like 'Who has done this before?' 'Who has information on this?'" says Callaghan. "And unless these people have the desire or the commission to go ask somewhere—and that is another issue—how do you ask, where do you ask? But unless they go look for it, it is very difficult to get them the knowledge or information."

SUMMARY TO PART TWO

Knowledge in action equals value. But value is a subjective concept. What is of value to one firm may not be to another. The first step in designing an effective transfer and KM system is to identify what is of value to *your* customers, and hence what is the driver of your own competitive advantage:

Is it customer intimacy? If so, you would want to center your efforts on identifying, capturing, and sharing knowledge and best practices about customers, developing and transferring knowledge and understanding of their needs, preferences, and businesses.

Is it leadership in product development? If so, you would want to reuse old designs, gain access to past experience in development, and make sure every bit of intelligence that could be useful to R&D flows across departmental silos and informs new designs.

Is it operational excellence? If so, you would encourage your employees to find, record, and share best practices in plants, business units, and other parts of your operations, across business units and geographic barriers, closing performance gaps, reducing producing costs, and improving performance overall.

Deciding where to focus your efforts is key. Why?

1. Although the principles of KM and transfer will not vary from one value proposition to the other, the types of knowledge and practices captures, and how they would be transferred most effectively, do.

2. A sharp focus helps target valuable resources on high-payoff areas.
3. It gets management attention.
4. It gets employees' attention—and heaven knows they've heard lots of improvement tales before.
5. Competition has never been more fierce nor response time shorter. We must respond and change *fast* and leverage every inch of existing assets.
6. The old-time emphasis on cost cutting is giving way to revenue growth.
7. Customers are becoming more sophisticated, and if you know your customers, you can figure out what they value the most.
8. You only have so much energy, resources, and time. Organizations only have so much tolerance for change. *Spend it wisely*.

Just which one of the three value propositions is best for your organization will depend on (1) where the greatest potential for improvement may be and (2) your firm's competitive strategy. But no matter what action you ultimately pursue, keep in mind that markets, business environment, customer preferences, and even your own operations are dynamic. Adapting your focus when the time comes is as critical as choosing the first course of action.

We can guarantee that exhortation to "Share more!" will not work. It takes systems and systematic approaches like internal benchmarking, mapping the knowledge terrain, capturing and summarizing of lessons learned, creating new practices. This costs money and time. And that is why having a *clear business* case and a *value proposition* is so important.

Remember that the best change and improvement techniques in the world are of little use without a clear idea of the value proposition and how knowledge and best practices can enhance it!

Part Three

THE FOUR ENABLERS OF TRANSFER

In the preceding sections, we laid the foundation for profitably leveraging the knowledge in your organization. The most effective way to share knowledge and best practices is through systematic transfer. The first step toward profitable management of your company's knowledge assets is choosing the right value proposition.

Part Three now focuses on creating the most supportive environment for transfer, by designing and aligning the enablers of transfer: culture, technology, infrastructure, and measurement. The following four chapters describe how each works, and how they all work together.

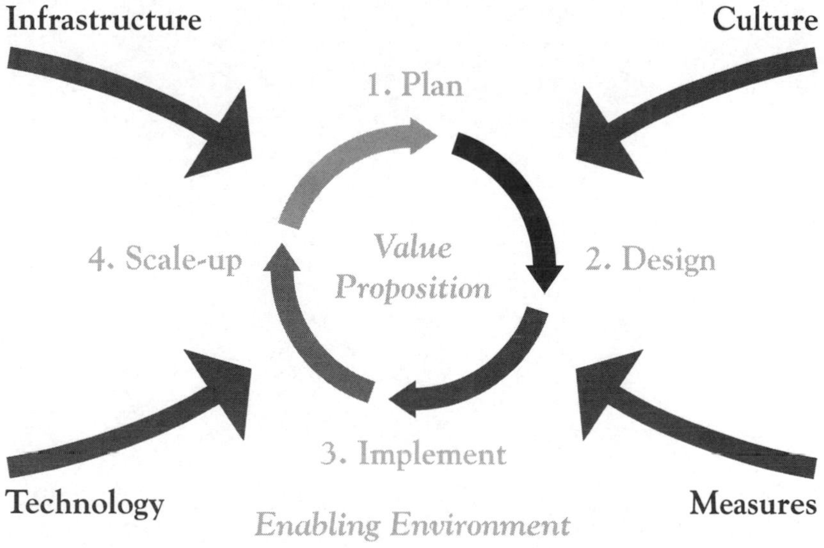

A Model for Best Practice Transfer

Chapter 9

CULTURE, THE UNSEEN HAND

> *Question: What are the three critical factors in knowledge management?*
> *Answer: Culture, culture, culture.*
> —*Bob Buckman, president, chairman, and CEO of Bulab Holdings, Inc.*

Infrastructure, culture, technology, and measurement are all necessary enablers; none alone is sufficient. Rather, they must all work in concert to achieve sustainable success.

But whereas all four are important—even critical—one is perhaps more potent and more difficult to alter. It yields less quickly or easily to innovation, because it is so much a function of your past. We are talking, of course, about an organization's culture. Each company has one. In fact, each division, even each department, has one.

Culture is the combination of shared history, expectations, unwritten rules, and social mores that affects the behavior of everyone, from managers to mailroom clerks. It's the set of underlying beliefs that, while never exactly articulated, are always there to color the perception of actions and communications. Whereas culture is the more ephemeral of enablers, it's arguably the most potent.

If your organization's natural tendency is to share and collaborate, all you have to do is eliminate structural barriers and provide enablers (like technology and facilitators) to allow practices and ideas to flow seamlessly across time and space. But if your company's nature is to hoard knowledge, then the best and greatest KM application may not be enough to alter your employees' behavior.

PEOPLE/CULTURE ARE THE KEY TO TRANSFER

Why?

First, because learning and sharing knowledge are *social activities*. They take place among people.

Second, *practices embedded in people, culture, and context are complex and rich*. Descriptions are thin and pale. (Think of the difference between a map and the journey itself.) Dialogue and demonstration can help enrich the learning.

A CULTURAL SELF-ASSESSMENT TEST

A PRO-SHARING CULTURE	AN ANTI-SHARING CULTURE
Learning through teaching and sharing	There are no incentives or sanctions to promote sharing of information and insights. Many incentives and support systems work against this concept.
Communal understanding through story telling	Staff feel they are constantly fighting the clock. Little time or attention is given to identifying lessons learned from projects.
Continuous exchange and creation of new knowledge—as experimentation occurs, people share and learn	Assumptions about projects or activities are not challenged.
Common areas of interest and expertise	Individuals are hired and promoted based on technical expertise.
Common issues and problems; strong professional ethics	Management and staff are reluctant to talk about projects that did not work well ("sharing your failure").
Personal relationships	The different missions and visions of divisions or departments produce different cultures that inhibit the transfer of knowledge and lessons learned.

Third, to ensure practices and knowledge not only transfer, but transfer effectively and make a difference, you have to *connect people* who can and are willing to share the deep, rich, tacit knowledge they have.

Across all cultures, mutual obligation is one of the most powerful social forces there is. Inside an organization, once people start helping and sharing with one another, the effort becomes a self-perpetuating cycle. We find that communities of practice and project teams are popping up in knowledge-managing organizations like so many mushrooms after the rain. They are the vehicles by which the rich, tacit knowledge gets shared among people who feel an obligation to help each other.

In fact, in his study of barriers to transfer, Gabriel Szulanski (1995) found that one of the strongest predictors of best practice transfer was the strength of the relationship between the source and recipient. The potential adopter of a best practice (the *recipient*) has to believe that the source is credible and knows what he or she is talking about. The *source* has to be generous enough to devote the counseling and communicating time the recipient needs in order to really understand, adapt, and implement practice.

Effective knowledge management requires creating a supportive, collaborative culture and eliminating traditional rivalries. Of course, all this assumes a basic level of modern organizational skills, such as collaborative work, using problem-solving paradigms, and effective listening. Organizations that haven't mastered these basic skills aren't going to be able to do business at all, probably. So knowledge management works best in healthy, sophisticated firms, or in small firms that have the luxury of starting out with such positive skills and norms.

LEVERAGING THE PEOPLE FACTOR

"Are you information-focused or people-focused?" asks KM expert Karl-Erik Sveiby of Queensland, Australia. "The choice of actions and the investment decisions that you will be comfortable with will be very different."

Both focuses can be called "knowledge management," but ultimately, says this expert, only one of them will be successful. "I believe that only a people-focused approach to KM will be competitive long-term, because at the end of the day, IT is readily available to everyone and any IT solution can easily be copied by the competition. Competitiveness rests in the tacit, not in the explicit."

Knowledge management practitioners are in agreement with Sveiby's premise. "In managing companies," says Roger Swanson, manager of corporate research services at Sequent Computers, "you've got to focus on values from the get-go. It's not unlike raising children. If you don't pay attention to the values in the early years, you're probably not going to like them very much when they become adults."

Even at companies that installed state-of-the-art IT infrastructure, the human aspect remains paramount. "We always run into the question, 'Is this work about databases?'" says Dave Ledet, director of shared learning at Amoco. "To some degree it is, but it is also very much about *establishing networks of people* across plants who share knowledge."

At the APQC, we've known for a very long time that a company's success is a function of the people that make it work. Call it organizational know-how, intellectual capital, or structural knowledge. Now, there is more recognition and empirical evidence to support this perspective.

A 1997 global study of the world's most admired companies, by *Fortune* magazine and the Hay Group, revealed a critical determinant of organization success. The study found that the world's elite organizations share *one thing* in common: They don't claim their people are their best asset. They act on it.

The world's most admired companies (among them Boeing, Microsoft, GE, FedEx, Pfizer, British Airways) are companies that take mission statements seriously. They attract successful people, use intense testing to pick the best of them, and then provide intense training to make sure they stay the best. These organizations view career development as an investment, not an expense; they promote internally, reward top performers, and make sure that their employees—these key stakeholders—are satisfied with their work. By so doing, they inspire a culture that recognizes the importance of people. And by recognizing the importance of people, they lay the groundwork for the critical task of leveraging their employees' experiences and practices.

THE KM MANAGER'S CULTURAL OVERHAUL "TO-DO" LIST

One could expect firms that have gone through numbers of management improvement initiatives to be skeptical of another new change effort; our research indicates that the opposite is true. And it's pretty easy to see why. Companies that have done a good deal of process improvement and quality work often already have in place the cross-functional communication and collaborative settings that are critical to sharing knowledge and know-how. (They also have other aspects of the infrastructure in place, as we will discuss in Chapter 11.)

ORGANIZATIONAL CAPABILITIES SUPPORTING TRANSFER

Through the 1980s and 1990s, competitive organizations spent much of their time developing capabilities that set the stage for a successful culture of sharing, transfer, and change. These capabilities include:

1. **a process improvement orientation**
2. **a common methodology for improvement and change**
3. **the ability to work effectively in teams**
4. **ability to capture learnings**
5. **technology to support cataloguing and collaboration**

Still, if you find yourself on the anti-sharing side of the table, or you believe your company's culture is one that's unlikely to nurture sharing, *do not stop reading here!* Cultural changes are possible, albeit difficult. To make them happen, there are at least *six* things you can do:

1. Believe People Want to Share

Call us eternal optimists, but from our experiences with a multitude of companies we know this to be true:

- People like to see their knowledge and expertise used, if we haven't created negative consequences
- People want to help their colleagues
- People want to learn from others they trust and respect

2. Prepare to Lead by Doing

Actions speak louder than words. And nowhere do they speak more loudly than in the arena of changing basic perceptions. The only way to make employees "believe" your vision is to act it—day in and day out. The impetus for success comes from the top.

Buckman and other KM and transfer pioneers strongly believe senior management must *participate* and *lead by sharing* to nurture the right cultural tone. For example, Buckman management avoids promoting anyone who is not recognized for sharing knowledge.

At Chevron, chairman and CEO Ken Derr believes it is senior management's role to see that people do not confuse power building with knowledge hoarding. Says Derr: "I think that a CEO should lead by example. This means participating and showing that you are personally committed to learning and the process of change. Whenever I visit with employee groups, I tell them sharing and using best practices is the single most important thing they can do."

"Knowledge management implies knowledge sharing and democracy, and if knowledge is a source of power it will be hoarded rather than shared," points out Onno van Ewyk, of HCI, a consulting firm in Sydney. "When executives create 'knowledge fiefdoms' this works against the interests of the company as a whole."

"Probably the *most important* thing that has allowed us to build a sharing strategy *is leadership support*," says Amoco's Dave Ledet. "Our president, Bill Lowrie, is adamant about Shared Learning. He talks about it constantly in his speeches and presentations. We are very fortunate in that we did not have to get leadership support. It was already there. That is what has allowed us to move forward at the speed we have." (See The view from the corner office, below.)

For many executives, the tallest challenge in instituting cultural changes may be giving up the notion that accumulating knowledge and keeping it from others is a source of power. In modern organizations, the most powerful individuals are those who inspire and lead by sharing. Instead of "command and control," executives have to "mentor and inspire."

Sometimes top executives truly want to share, but simply don't know how. At Texas Instruments, Cindy Johnson has been spending a lot of her time talking to top managers about how to share the lessons of their daily experiences with "the troops."

3. Rely on the Twin Forces of Capitalism and Democracy

As a nation, we swear by them, both capitalism and democracy. We live by them. We even fight for them. As companies, we rarely do. "The biggest problem in most organizations is that they are centrally planned economies," Professor Hallal of George Washington University noted in a personal interview.

Creating a free-enterprise system which accurately reflects economic reality, on an intrafirm basis, breeds accountability. Accountability drives the need for knowledge. When people *need* the knowledge, they tend to trade it and *share it*.

> **THE VIEW FROM THE CORNER OFFICE**
>
> **Many executives from companies profiled here have been quite vocal about the power of shared learning and transfer:**
>
> **Our behavior is driven by a fundamental core belief: the desire and the ability of an organization to continuously learn from any source, and to rapidly convert this learning into action is its ultimate competitive advantage.**
>
> **—Jack Welch, CEO, General Electric**
>
> **Shared Learning is an amazing concept. It allows the corporation to cash in on what we already have invested in: the knowledge and experience of our talented people. It gives us the ability to continually harvest a crop of innovative solutions and creative applications. It's essential that we accept the challenge of figuring out how to make the necessary investments so that Shared Learning will secure a place at the core of Amoco culture.**
>
> **—William Lowrie, president, Amoco Corporation**
>
> **The most powerful individuals will be those who do the best job of transferring knowledge to others. . . . Frankly, I do not think you can have a successful knowledge transfer effort without that proactive entrepreneurial support from the top.**
>
> **—Bob Buckman, president, chairman, and CEO, Bulab Holdings, Inc.**

SEQUENT'S KNOWLEDGE ECONOMY

Nowhere is the notion of a free-enterprise knowledge system more clearly illustrated than in the "knowledge economy" transfer system established by Sequent Computer Systems, Inc. "It always amazes me that we want capitalism everywhere but inside our own firms," notes Marc Demarest, ex-CKO of Sequent. Sequent used two overriding metaphors in designing its transfer initiatives:

1. "We are supporting and nurturing a knowledge economy, and we want it to be a capitalist one."
2. "We are managing a 'city' of knowledge, and as city managers we are not in the business of telling merchants what they ought to be selling."

Sequent does not offer specific rewards and incentives to transfer system participants. "In our knowledge economy, we encourage and reward publishers, by using their materials and most importantly by attributing 'expertise' to those publishers when use events produce desirable economic results for the user," explains Demarest.

The value and relevancy of knowledge is *always* in the eye of the beholder. "Is information relevant? Relevant to whom? Under what circumstances? For what purposes? The whole point of KM is that no one—most definitely not some wonk with the title CKO in a headquarters office somewhere—is in a position to understand the hundreds of different, specific contexts in which knowledge is required to satisfy a customer or business partner," says Demarest. "We teach producers to think about their consumers: their needs, their roles, the processes in which they participate; we teach consumers to reassemble componentized knowledge into precisely the tools they need at precisely the time they need them; and we teach them to discipline publishers who produce poorly formed, unusable, or toxic components."

"We see ourselves as a knowledge economy within a city of knowledge: producers and consumers meeting and exchanging value in a (largely electronic) marketplace," explains Demarest. Whereas such laissez-faire approach may not work in an organization that is accustomed to planned economics, this model of distributed responsibility has proved so far to be the only one that works within Sequent.

4. Develop Collaborative Relationships

Collaborative relationships enable tacit knowledge and high-value practices to transfer. That's the stuff you cannot put on the information systems. From teams to communities of practice, these basic units of innovation and collaboration bring together like-minded people and people with a shared goal. Projects to transfer best practices, such as the Chevron Best Practices teams, are one vehicle to create these relationships.

5. Instill Personal Responsibility for Knowledge Creation and Sharing

If people are the engine of knowledge, they should be responsible for identifying, maintaining, expanding, and sharing their knowledge base. The profitability and viability of enterprises are directly related to the degree to which people are able to act intelligently in all situations. A successful future depends upon the extent to which each individual builds, shares, and applies his or her knowledge.

ON SPACE AND SHARING

Sometimes, just making sure office space and architectural design match the desired collaborative atmosphere can go along way. One sure way to tell the cultural bent of an organization is to count the number of shut office doors and the available "communal space." If there is no "coffee room," the chances that people will informally interconnect are slim. If most doors are closed, you may rightly wonder what people may be hiding, or hiding from.

Soon after forming, the World Bank's Education Knowledge Management System (EKMS) (see case study in Chapter 16) had the opportunity to move to an open office space designed to stimulate team building. The staff agreed to move in for a six-to-eight-week trial period to see how the alternative environment affected their work. The new area had no walls, it organized the staff in teams, and put them close to each other; it also included several common areas. "The open office has made a real difference," says Martha Pattillo-Siv, coordinator for the Education Advisory Service. "There is a lot of spontaneity in this atmosphere." The upshot: The staff is *not* asking to go back to the old office arrangement.

This philosophy is in line with a new type of social contract between employees and the firm: Employees are responsible for their growth, and the firm is responsible for providing them with an opportunity and the tools to grow. This contract *has to be two-sided*. If you require personal responsibility but provide nothing in return, employees are going to balk at cooperating, as well they should.

For example, at USAA—a firm believer in personal responsibility for knowledge—displaced employees are retrained, not fired. Turnover is less than 6 percent for the whole organization. In return, USAA expects employees to make themselves "continuously employable." And it works!

This "pull" philosophy puts the responsibility with employees to

TI'S THREE-TIER APPROACH TO CULTURE

Some companies know they have to start from scratch. Others are lucky enough to have the basic cultural ingredients. When Texas Instruments began its best-practice transfer initiative in 1994, it was certainly among the lucky ones.

"My job has been really relatively easy," confesses Cindy Johnson of TI. "We have had strong leadership in place, as well as a strong process of teaming and a true customer focus. We had the culture to begin with." Even so, it took work, and a combination of senior management and transfer team efforts to ensure culture and knowledge management fit snugly together.

According to Johnson, there are three layers to the development of a sharing culture: "You have to provide *purpose and motivation*; you have to provide the *tools* and finally, you have to complement both with a *reward and incentive structure*." (These tools are detailed extensively in the TI case study in Part Four.)

TI's transfer efforts took off in earnest in 1994, after top management formulated a new vision and initiated a focused movement toward building a companywide sense of purpose. That vision, *for leadership in digital solutions to drive the network society,* resonated throughout TI's global operations. "It's been our battle cry," says Johnson. "And it has driven the effort to create new business and adopt new technologies more quickly."

In addition to formulating the grand vision, "the role of top management is to model the behavior," says Johnson. "CEOs spend the bulk of

seek out knowledge to improve the performance of themselves and their processes. According to all our research at the APQC, this "pull" approach to knowledge sharing is essential for long-term success. While some knowledge and practices can be "pushed," the active quest inspired by "pulling" indicates a desire for learning which is a prerequisite for successful transfer (more on these "prerequisites" in Part Five of this book).

6. Create a Collective Sense of Purpose

Communities of practice and project teams share on a "micro" basis to help meet common needs and goals. Similarly, company-wide sharing

their time learning and connecting with other people." "They talk to customers, financial organizations, government/regulatory bodies, other business leaders to learn about what works and what doesn't and understand the business environment. Basically, they should want all of their people to do the same for their respective areas."

Easier said than done. Whereas most senior managers practice knowledge management in "private," they rarely see the benefit of publicizing their daily activities. "They should make it very obvious that what they're doing is really about learning and applying the learning to the business," says Johnson. "Most of them think this should be very apparent to everyone. But it isn't!"

Often, the failure to share is not intentional. "People who are very good at something are frequently the last ones to show up when they're most needed," notes Johnson. For example, a thin person is unlikely to attend a weight loss class; however, he or she may have best practices in weight loss. And sometimes people don't know what they did to become good. They need help recognizing and understanding *how* they've become successful before they can share their best practices.

While TI's top management was busy creating a vision and leading the transfer initiatives, Johnson's group was charged with providing the supportive systems and creating reward schemes that encourage transfer. "It's a fine balance," admits the veteran transfer expert. Rewarding transfer activities specifically may work initially. But ultimately, the organization must change its overall promotional compensation scheme to align it with new values.

must be inspired by a common goal. A vision. A sense of social and organizational purpose that defines the raison d'être of the entity. Knowledge and practices are meaningless if not put in context of "purpose" and surrounded by a set of overriding values. Without them, it becomes nearly impossible to enlist people's cooperation and enthusiasm.

"We're here to make money" is *not good enough*. The common goal must be both more specific than that (in terms of industry/product leadership), and more inspiring than that (including some social relevancy). Working together to achieve a common objective, whether on a division basis or on a global, enterprise-wide basis, for a common goal is the safest way of ensuring a culture that's bent on sharing.

TO REWARD OR NOT TO REWARD, THAT IS THE QUESTION

In all three of APQC's large-scale studies on knowledge management, we reached similar conclusions about the role of rewards: if the process of sharing and transfer is not inherently rewarding, celebrated, and supported by the culture, then artificial rewards won't have much effect, and can make people cynical.

Reflecting the importance of embedding knowledge management tools and transfer processes into the work itself, we continue to find a *greater use of intangible* versus tangible rewards for engaging in transfer activities.

A good transfer system should provide intrinsic rewards to the professionals who use it. For example, does such a system let its users better, more easily, and more efficiently achieve their project and work objectives; do they receive more peer recognition as key contributors and experts; and is their work faster, richer, and more rewarding?

Explicit rewards and incentives go only so far. After years of studying corporate incentives schemes, we've reached the following *firm* conclusion: If the practice helps people do their work, they will share.

- At *The World Bank*, the Africa Live Database provides incentive to update data because analysts become more effective.
- At *Sequent Computer Systems, Inc.*, sales and marketing teams know they can quickly find the best advice, sales presentations, system solutions, and customer and competitive information by accessing the KM system.

- At *Arthur Andersen LLP,* consultants can rapidly get the training and content they need to be successful in client engagements.

Think about e-mail. It has exploded onto the scene and caught like fire both at work and at home. Does anyone offer workers big rewards for using e-mail? No. They know intuitively that it helps them do their work better. Telling everybody that between 5 and 6 P.M. they should be contributing knowledge, and that if they do, they will get a mouse pad, won't change the way people work.

Not surprisingly, we find that only a minority of firms use formal financial rewards to promote sharing behaviors. Instead, successful firms place a big focus on a personal responsibility strategy, and embedding knowledge development and transfer into their employees' professional and career development systems.

Price Waterhouse is a good example of how a consulting firm can encourage knowledge creation and transfer. In the past, the blue-chip accounting firm's promotions were based on seniority and tenure, not excellence and mentoring. In the mid-1990s, Price Waterhouse added knowledge sharing to its performance appraisal system to ensure that employees' efforts to share with others are recognized in their career path and compensation. Employees must be able to produce "evidence" of actual knowledge sharing such as tutoring/training, development of methodology, publishing and presenting on topics, coaching and mentoring, and so on.

RECOGNITION AS THE CURRENCY OF CHOICE

People want their expertise and knowledge to be used—and acknowledged. Individual recognition is how organizations have traditionally met this need, and that will continue. But if companies want to encourage sharing, they need to recognize and celebrate that behavior as well. Texas Instruments created the NIHBIDIA Award: Not Invented Here But I Did It Anyway.

Begun in 1996, TI's annual sharing day (ShareFair, where all the best practice teams man booths to publicize and answer questions about their practices) culminates in an award ceremony for those organizations that have most successfully shared best practices and knowledge—and produced great results. Both organizations (and sometimes there are more than two involved) receive an award from senior executives for collaborating on the exchange of best practices. This is a highly prestigious award at TI, because it reinforces *both* the process *and* the results.

STRUCTURING A REWARD SYSTEM: A CHECKLIST

When creating your own knowledge management and transfer reward and recognition system, keep these points in mind:

1. Recognition lies in being perceived as an expert by employees and management. Ensure that an internal expert's name is attached to documents, guidelines, and presentations they created.
2. Using the knowledge system has to be self-rewarding to the consumer; users have to get something out of it, be it knowledge they need or a sense of status and recognition.
3. Time to use and create knowledge has to be recognized and rewarded; if participants feel that have to "steal" time from the "real" work to do this—they won't.
4. Formal rewards may be demeaning to professionals; don't give cash bonuses to people motivated by a sense of involvement and contribution.
5. Create recognition for transferring and using best practices; you can do that by celebrating best practice success stories, and propagating tales of big savings and important contributions.
6. Recognize both parties or units involved in the transfer; at any given time, an employee is contributing or receiving knowledge. If both ends are not feeling rewarded, you'll run out of content pretty quickly.
7. A "standardized" reward system will help institutionalize the practice into the common culture.

To repeat, if the transfer activity helps employees achieve their overall goals, they will pursue it. Hence rewards and recognition may be healthy and useful in the early stages of building enthusiasm for transfer. However, in the long run and for a sustainable effort, employees have to find *the work itself* rewarding.

Chapter 10

USING INFORMATION TECHNOLOGY TO SUPPORT KNOWLEDGE TRANSFER

Technology has given us new ways to keep in touch with each other and share information. We have to take advantage of that technology to get better, faster.

—Bill Baker, Texas Instruments

It is no coincidence that information technology (IT) has blossomed at the same time that knowledge is becoming recognized as the most valuable of a firm's assets. There is a powerful synergistic relationship between KM and technology; that relationship drives increasing returns and increasing sophistication on both fronts. As information technology has become our personal desktop tool and our link to each other, we have grown to covet even more access to information and other people's knowledge. In turn, we demand ever better and more effective IT tools, ones that become part of the way we work.

A SYNERGISTIC RELATIONSHIP

We use the term *synergy*; other experts have other ways to describe the relationship between technology and knowledge management. Noted

KM expert Karl Eric Sveiby has described IT systems as "hygiene factors." "IT is for KM like a bathroom is for a house buyer," says Sveiby. "Essential because without it the house is not even considered by buyers. But the bathroom is generally not the vital differentiating factor for the buyer."

Hygienic or synergistic, take your pick. The key is that the rise of distributed technologies like intranets and Lotus Notes has had critical implications for knowledge managers—and not all of them are positive. (See page 93). On the one hand, IT has reduced the cost and sped up the process of transferring best practices and knowledge. On the other, IT has led, in many cases, to a flood of information (*not* knowledge—note the distinction here!) that has seriously overloaded employees' capacity to make sense of their environment.

"Technology has made it realistic to globally share knowledge," says Cindy Johnson at TI. "Before, it was very expensive, slow, and tedious. We could create enormous repositories, but we would never get anything out of them." With search engines and browsers, the process of delving into knowledge repositories has become both simplified and faster.

At the same time, however, these technologies have exponentially increased the amount and speed of information, often leading to organizational paralysis—a disease that occurs when a swelling amount of information is chasing a shrinking number of brains. When the human capacity to absorb and make sense is exceeded, managers cannot make decisions and employees don't know where to get quick answers to their customers' questions.

"Over ten years ago, when electronic information just started to show up from external and internal sources, the initial problem was getting access and organizing the information," says Bipin Junnarkar at Monsanto. But not anymore. Now, the problem is getting the right information to the right people, at the right time.

So, while the explosive growth and ready adoption of Internet and intranet technologies has been an enormous catalyst for knowledge sharing, just throwing IT solutions at the knowledge management challenge is not going to do it. *IT makes connection possible, but does not make it happen.* Buying systems and implementing state-of-the-art architectures does not, in itself, guarantee the sharing of best practices and know-how. Sometimes, too much technology or the wrong type of technology can hurt KM efforts.

SHARING-ENABLING TECHNOLOGIES MAY NOT BE NEW, BUT . . .

There's nothing totally new about the use of technology to help "spread the word." Communications technologies have been helping us share stories, events, and experiences since our tribal days. Even in modern times, we've been leveraging IT to manipulate and share knowledge, going back to the telephone, faxes, and even Artificial Intelligence in the 1950s. So what's changed?

The answer is in the pervasive use of groupware and Internet/intranet technologies.

Every new "technology" follows a similar path: One person buys, say, a color television. Then the next. Then the whole neighborhood. And before long, no one you know still uses a black-and-white TV. Tools that work become pervasive. Once they do, their "installed base" perpetuates and enhances their usefulness. What use is a telephone if you're the only one who has it? Same with Lotus Notes and intranet technologies—but with an added benefit: The telephone, or even e-mail, does not "record" and "detail" our practices and experiences. The stories are told. And once they're told, they are gone. They cannot be searched, consulted, remembered, shared, and expanded. The reasons intranets and Lotus Notes work for knowledge management is that they combine organized retrieval with ubiquitous access. Retrieval and access. That's half the solution.

The other half is not technology—it's people. So although this chapter focuses on IT, we have to reiterate that technology is not the solution; it is part of the solution. Technology is necessary but not sufficient to make transfer happen. The popular slogan is "Build it so they will come." Our slight amendment is: "If you build it, they will come, but only for e-mail."

If you are going to be successful, you need the technology in place; it's got to be good and it's got to be easy to use. However, as our friend Tom Davenport says, "If you're spending more than one third of your energy on the technology side, you're probably not going to be successful."

Ultimately, knowledge and best practices are in people's heads. The behavioral aspects of the system are therefore more important than its architecture. "The world is littered with the remains of KM programs that companies built and then nobody came," says Davenport. You don't want to be among them.

KM/IT RULES OF THUMB

Tom Davenport uses the "stay under a one-third of resources" litmus test to ensure IT does not become "the be all and end all" of KM. We offer two other helpful rules of thumb:

1. *The more "valuable" the knowledge, the less sophisticated the technology that supports it.* Here's how it works: Databases and datamining tools, for example, are high on the technological sophistication scale. The knowledge they contain, however, is truly low-grade. In fact, databases *do not contain knowledge* at all. They contain *data.* In contrast, help desks, equipped with nothing more than humans and telephones, are low-tech but offer a very high knowledge value. Hence, the higher the grade of knowledge, the lower-tech the solution. The two are inversely correlated.
2. *Tacit knowledge is best shared through people; explicit knowledge can be shared through machines. Or, the more tacit the knowledge, the less high-tech the solution.* If you take the continuum between tacit and explicit knowledge (from totally tacit, poorly organized, somewhat documented, to highly documented and organized explicit knowledge), the more explicit the knowledge, the more it lends itself to high-tech solutions. Tacit know-how, meanwhile, is often best transferred via people or "help desks." For example, when the World Bank began to organize a sharing mechanism for its tacit and poorly organized explicit knowledge, it set up discussion groups and help desks to help transfer best practices, instead of trying to document them in some mega database.

BUILDING THE TRANSFER PLATFORM

Let's review what we've said so far:

- IT and KM have a *symbiotic relationship*.
- Companies must be careful *not to confuse databases with knowledge management*. New technologies are certainly enabling and catalytic (in particular Notes and intranets), but they *are not a solution* in and of themselves.
- Technology may not be the most important component of KM, but try doing without it and you will quickly discover the limits of lunch clubs and informal get-togethers.
- Finally, IT has to be used with intelligence, *matching knowledge types and needs with the right IT applications*.

You may not need the latest and greatest IT to get your transfer efforts going. But you will need a *standardized* company-wide architecture to ensure the sustainability and scalability of those efforts. Perhaps unlike any other area of technological design, knowledge and best practice sharing cannot take place if companies allow the proliferation of separate systems and "IT archipelagoes"—i.e., department-specific programs. If a firm does not have the architecture of an organization-wide solution in mind when designing local KM/IT solutions, then the organization will, over time, face problems in integration and scalability; subsequently, it stands to lose much of the leverage knowledge management can create.

KNOWLEDGE-ENABLED INTRANETS

Most companies today have already figured out their basic information technology architecture for other reasons (such as the Year 2000 problem or enterprise-wide computing needs). Typical choices involve corporate intranets and Web-based technologies, supported by collaborative groupware and database applications. However, whereas most of this basic IT infrastructure is either already in place or rapidly coming on-line inside organizations, the real challenge is in deciding how the actual knowledge management applications will be used and maintained.

Here are a few helpful guidelines to help ensure your intranet-based KM solution achieves its purpose:

1. Understand the business purpose for what you are trying to accomplish—define the objectives.
2. Determine whether the current technology can be adapted or can be purchased off the shelf.
3. Assess the ability of the physical infrastructure currently in place to handle the kind and quantity of traffic moving around on the intranet.
4. Identify internal support requirements for maintenance of the system.
5. Organize your content; there may be a need for librarians.
6. Choose a central location for your Web site, from which one can navigate to any other area. If you select a decentralized location instead, think about issues surrounding policies and procedures, training, and redundancies in processes and information.
7. Design for ease of use—intranet and Web-based solutions are almost training-free in terms of the technology.
8. Facilitate universal access and universal use.
9. Consider initial costs, including shareware and software, as well as secondary costs, which can include training, operations and management, increased bandwidth installations, lost productivity due to obsessive use of Web content creation tools, and fruitless forays into Web junkyards.

Few of the decisions associated with intranet implementation are brand new. So practice what you preach and don't cast off learnings from implementing on-line transaction processing systems or decision support systems. They all apply here.

INTRANETS EMPOWER SHARING EFFORTS

At *Arthur Andersen*, KnowledgeSpace℠ (an intranet-based application) now integrates various legacy databases and information sources into a "one-stop shop" for the information used to perform AA's business, including content from a Global Best Practice database.

THE BENEFITS OF K-ENABLED INTRANETS

The benefits of knowledge-enabled intranets are numerous. They include:

- ***Lower communication costs,*** **driven by reducing expenses related to printing, mailing, and processing of documents.**
- ***Improved productivity*** **by making information more widely and quickly accessible.**
- ***Higher team productivity,*** **created through collaborative work environments.**
- ***Rapid implementation*** **as a result of open protocol standards.**
- ***Relatively low costs for hardware and software.***

At *National Semiconductor,* the knowledge-enabled intranet began as a grass-roots effort with the development of its first Web pages in August 1994. Since then, it has expanded beyond departmental home pages to encompass enterprise-wide services such as employee directory services, teams and communities of practice, research and development findings for new product development, and staffing/career opportunities. The intranet is also used for day-to-day activities such as scheduling conference room usage and placing orders ranging from office supplies to assembly/fab supplies.

At *Buckman Laboratories,* web-based forums and the global infrastructure provided by CompuServe have allowed associates to access project tracking systems, customer relationship management systems, groupware, bulletin boards, virtual conference rooms, and databases that capture institutional memory twenty-four hours a day.

At *Sequent Computer Systems,* the Sequent Corporate Electronic Library (SCEL) is implemented as a combination of services using database management systems, full-text retrieval engines, file system storage, and complex clusters of programs, all of which are integrated into Sequent's worldwide intranet and all of which are accessible through consumers' Web browsers. The external Internet, as well as core online transaction processing and decision support systems, are integrated into this infrastructure.

COLLABORATIVE TOOLS AND GROUPWARE

More and more companies are turning to the Web-centric model as a way of encouraging cross-enterprise collaboration, but sometimes a more advanced tool such as groupware works better. That's mostly the case for more advanced and structured documents sharing.

Collaborative tools, such as groupware, have been around since 1989 and focus primarily on communication—individual, group, project, or companywide. Groupware supports work groups and people working together. Lotus Notes is the most prevalent example. Knowledge managers use collaborative tools for a variety of reasons, ranging from e-mail to the sharing of factual knowledge.

Most companies with Lotus Notes combine it with an intranet to allow both structured and free-flow sharing.

For example, at *Buckman*, LearningSpace from Lotus has been added to the KM application suite to facilitate the company's distance learning project. LearningSpace is a distributive learning tool with interconnected networks of Notes databases and a structured training model. Its purpose is to deliver asynchronous, just-in-time (yet standardized) education and training to associates throughout the world.

National Semiconductor uses Windows 95 as a base infrastructure with Lotus Notes as an e-mail and knowledge-sharing tool. Lotus Notes is installed on more than 5,000 desktops. The field sales group has been using Lotus Notes for the past few years to share customer data. The mainframe e-mail system is being transferred to Notes, which will provide an opportunity for a wide variety of people to use National Semiconductor's knowledge-sharing technology.

Texas Instruments placed its core Best Practices KnowledgeBase on Notes in March of 1995. The original facilitators, the Best Practice Sharing Team, and the Quality Leadership Team loaded the original supply of best practices; to date, the database contains more than 500 practices.

The *World Bank* relies on Lotus Notes to help its traveling staff members to stay in touch when on missions. Each notebook computer will contain a Lotus Notes–based knowledge management navigation system. This way, staff members can stay up to date no matter where and how long their mission lasts.

BOB BUCKMAN'S IDEA-SHARING SYSTEM

Bob Buckman envisioned the characteristics of an ideal electronic network, and developed the following design features for it, presaging by ten years the characteristics of effective "knowledge management" systems.

1. **Keep the number of transfer steps in the transmission between individuals to one to alleviate the potential distortion of knowledge.**
2. **Allow all employees access to the system.**
3. **Allow all employees to make contributions.**
4. **Make the system available from any location, twenty-four hours a day.**
5. **Have a user-friendly system able to search on every word.**
6. **Allow the users to contribute in their native language and where deemed appropriate provide the required translation.**
7. **Provide a system that updates automatically as information is provided.**

NOTES VS. THE INTRANET

Notes and the intranet are both potent sharing tools; however, they will not do your work for you. Don't be lured into thinking that mere installation of an intranet or a Lotus Notes implementation will make everyone want to share.

The success of the KM application of your choice is dependent on the human infrastructure or the soft side of knowledge management for its success. The soft side is often the most difficult piece. (See Chapter 9.)

The good news however is that whereas, in the past, companies needed to make a choice to go with Notes *or* an intranet architecture, that's no longer necessary. Although the debate still rages about which "architecture" is the most knowledge-inclined, most users end up combining them and rely on Domino to allow access back and forth.

Some companies, like Sequent, swear by the intranet as the quintessential KM application. Its very "spirit," they argue, is about sharing, and no one "owns" it, hence your migration path is not tied to a particular vendor's plans. True enough. On the other hand, Notes provides an environment for more sophisticated collaboration and structure exchanges. The trick is choosing the best technology for the specific KM

INTRANETS MEAN ROI

In 1997, The Meta Group Inc., a market research and consultancy in Stamford, Connecticut, analyzed the return on investment (ROI) of intranet applications. According to Meta, 80 percent of companies surveyed generated a positive ROI, with an average annualized return of 38 percent.

Meta surveyed 55 companies, ranging in size from $2 million to $35 billion, and employing intranet technologies across a broad range of applications, including collaboration, customer service, inventory management, and database access. By and large, applications that were interactive and affected the firms' value chain directly yielded much higher ROIs. Meta also found that the culture of the company and its IT department have a significant impact on the success or failure of intranet technology.

effort. Neither one is necessarily better than the other. But in any event, Notes and intranets should be used with discretion.

FROM BACKBONE TO BODY—TOOLS AND APPLICATIONS

If the greatest database in the company is housed in the individual minds of the associates of the organization, then that is where the power of the organization resides. These individual knowledge bases are continually changing and adapting to the real world in front of them. We have to connect these individual knowledge bases together so that they can do whatever they do best in the shortest possible time.
—Bob Buckman, president, chairman, and CEO, Bulab Holdings, Inc.

If Notes and/or the intranet are the technological backbone of the transfer process, then this backbone holds a complex body of KM-specific tools and applications that enable particular aspects of sharing.

Two broad classes of IT applications are being used to support transfer, and each contains a number of tools specific to the application:

1. Knowledge Transfer and Exchange
    - Structured document repositories (a.k.a. databases)
    - Discussion databases

- Pointers to expertise
- Document exchange and video infrastructure

2. Data Analysis and Performance Support
   - Performance support systems
   - Problem resolution systems
   - Data-to-knowledge conversion systems
     —Data mining
     —Decision support
     —Real-time intelligent data analysis

We will focus on the first group here, primarily because it reflects the market's focus and practice. In our 1997 study "Using Information Technology to Support Knowledge Management" (APQC, 1997), 89 percent of participants indicated that their goal was to capture and transfer knowledge and best practices, not analyze data.

Furthermore, data analysis and performance support applications involve distinctly different and highly specialized technologies and design considerations. Such tools are applied to raw data and/or information, not knowledge, so they fall outside our best-practice focus.

Still, we believe there may be a vast potential for combining the two areas into a holistic knowledge and practice sharing system. To that end, we encourage readers to find out more about data analysis and decision support, and provide a few thoughts/examples (see page 100, KM's Uncharted Territory).

TRANSFERRING VIA STRUCTURED DOCUMENT REPOSITORIES

Structured document repositories typically contain databases that have structured content consisting of regular, alphanumeric data capable of being stored in conventional relational databases. A good example is *best practices databases*, which are usually repositories of short descriptions of best practices and/or pointers to contacts within the organization who have knowledge about these practices.

Databases that are organized around customers—which may include information about customer inquiries, needs, and interactions—and databases containing competitor intelligence may also be stored in these repositories. These databases typically include sales presentations, reports, engagement information, competitor analysis, and external feeds.

The following three tips may be helpful when implementing structured document repositories:

1. It is important to supply "magnet content" that causes people to use the database in the context of their work.
2. The best systems automatically capture content rather than requiring people to take an extra step to reenter it.
3. Every system needs a disciplined process for creation, evaluation, categorization, maintenance, and renewal—that is, people have to be assigned these responsibilities.

At the *World Bank*, the Africa Region Live Database (LDB) provides data and analytical tools to country and sector economists, who are then responsible for maintaining the quality and timeliness of data. The analytical tools are closely adapted to the work needs of the economists. They are offered as an inducement to economists to do their work within the LDB and to perform the data maintenance.

One of the ways the *Sequent Corporate Electronic Library* is supplied with valuable information is through the hypermail approach. This simple technology retains e-mail exchanges and organizes them by "threads" or subject so that others can search/find them in the future. Instead of re-inputting solutions as new documents, the learnings are automatically captured and catalogued.

TRANSFERRING VIA DISCUSSION DATABASES

These are discussion groups of project or work teams (whether e-mail listsserves, news groups, or Lotus Notes–based discussion groups). They may also support *communities of practice*, *project work teams*, and salespeople or sales and *marketing teams*.

Helpful implementation tips include:

1. Make sure you have shared norms.
2. Provide some payback for participation (tangible or intangible).
3. Ensure active facilitation by a moderator.
4. Offer a "one stop" solution for e-mail and discussion.
5. Nourish the on-line community through other means as well (e.g., face-to-face meetings).

6. Remember that content has to be good, if these are to attract visitors.
7. Use logical, intuitive structure for views.
8. Use library scientists who understand the technology, and technologists who understand library science.
9. Provide some editorial and publishing support to increase value and accuracy.
10. Create automatic systems for "cleaning out the closet" and archiving past discussions.

Sequent has two kinds of mechanisms for discussion: NetNews and group distribution lists. These discussion groups may be created by any employee, archived at the request of an employee, and either moderated or not, as the community using it chooses. Employees can add themselves to, and remove themselves from, discussions at will when the discussion group is not moderated, and by permission of the moderator when moderated.

Texas Instruments implemented a discussion database through Lotus Notes, enabling employees to communicate business gaps and solutions. Externally identified best practices and benchmarking information also were incorporated into the Best Practices KnowledgeBase.

AA OnLine is *Arthur Andersen's* firmwide conferencing forum designed to help its professionals stay informed about industry and service-line issues and communicate with other firm members. AA OnLine is an interactive conferencing tool that provides users with the means to talk electronically to a large group of people and the ability to share resources and expertise. The database is organized around "groups" or knowledge networks, which are defined as communities of practice with a need to share valuable materials or ideas. AA OnLine is currently deployed throughout the firm and hosts announcements and discussions; it holds resources for about eighty-plus AA knowledge networks. There are currently 20,000 users.

TRANSFERRING VIA POINTERS TO EXPERTISE

Pointer systems are applications such as "yellow pages" of internal experts, project managers, or interested parties. They may also include human resource (HR) listings and profiles of employees. While these are technologically simple, and extremely effective in enabling the transfer of high-value knowledge, they are not as simple to implement.

When building a pointer system, use the following guidelines:

1. Do not rely on users to maintain their own HR information.
2. Information needs to interface or be fed by the corporate HR information system.
3. Maps of experts and communities of practice are at times out of date but are better than nothing.
4. Formal discussion groups can be catalogued.
5. Experts must be motivated to supply their profiles.
6. "Expert" may be a highly political concept.
7. Don't create a pointer system that's basically an electronic version of a phone book. Add value by interconnecting the yellow pages with other components of the KM application suite, so that users can use "hotlinks" to further refine their needs.
8. Make sure there's a simple and standard format to follow for new submissions and revisions.

Teltech Resource Network Corporation, a company based in Minneapolis, has made the corporate yellow pages its core business. Teltech specializes in putting together networks of technical experts and helps its clients search for the right expert. In fact, Teltech has been so successful it has taken the lessons it learned from building its own business and is now helping others design and create knowledge and transfer systems with an emphasis on the human connection. "The most immediate payback [for KM effort] is through creating the navigation capabilities to put people in touch with people," says Andy Michuda, Teltech's president and CEO. Indeed, he says, he's "seeing more and more companies initially focused on computers and technology now starting to migrate to people-based capabilities." What these companies realize is that it's not all about systems. "From a process standpoint, the key is to find the pockets of intellectual capital and bring them together in a timely manner."

At *Sequent*, the corporate yellow pages are provided by integrating SCEL with PeopleSoft, Sequent's on-line HR system, which allows dynamic access to personnel profiles maintained by the HR systems.

Subject matter expertise is advertised through "professional profiles" maintained by employees. Sequent Computer Systems planned to implement a corporate skills repository in the HR organization in 1998. That repository would be integrated into, and accessible from, SCEL.

TRANSFERRING VIA DOCUMENT EXCHANGE AND VIDEO

E-mail is the most pervasive and effective means of electronic communication and collaboration. It is real-time, fast, easy, and user-driven. Video conferencing is growing, but not ubiquitous from the desktop, like e-mail. Though e-mail is a rich source of information, there is too much of it and it is unfiltered—thus, gems are frequently lost.

At *Sequent*, e-mail and news groups are provided using the same underlying technology suite (TCP/IP and Internet protocols) as SCEL. News groups are accessible through the browser's built-in news-reading capability. E-mail discussions on shared aliases are treated as documents by SCEL and archived for future reference by interested consumers.

At CIGNA *Property & Casualty*, when an underwriter gains insight on a topic, he or she only needs to push a "shared observation" button to immediately transfer the comments as an e-mail, which allows the underwriter to communicate with other underwriters in the network.

THE ROLE OF THE IT ORGANIZATION

It's time to stop and take a breather.

We've run through pages of examples, lists of tools and applications, helpful tips and implementation guides. Certainly lots of trees. But do you see the forest?

In addressing the technological aspect of knowledge management, we address more than the technology platforms and applications. We also have to address strategy and underlying paradigms that drive the design, as well as the roles of people throughout the system. We've talked about the backbone/platform, we talked about the parts of the "body." Now, we talk about the neural networks that make it all work in sync.

One of the most important characteristics of a knowledge management architecture is that structures and roles are never static. In a knowledge-intensive economy and organization, it is not surprising that managing knowledge requires that people be specifically assigned to every stage in the process—collecting, organizing, adding value, disseminating, and supporting knowledge-in-use. Four-fifths of productive value added by technical change will continue to result not from

KM'S UNCHARTED TERRITORY

We may know more about using technology to enable transfer than we know about data analysis and performance support. But in our travels throughout the KM landscape, we happened to find several examples of such applications that certainly fall within the boundaries of knowledge management.

Data analysis and performance support applications are usually found within the business units supporting the actual work processes. These applications include the following:

- **performance support systems**
- **problem resolution systems**
- **data-to-knowledge conversion systems, including data mining, decision support, and real-time intelligent data analysis**

***Performance Support Systems*. Used in real time to support the individual's job performance and learning, these types of systems usually:**

- **support a broader set of process and strategic objectives**
- **require significant training and retraining to use**
- **relate to specific processes or functions**

Sales and call center support systems are a good example of this type of application. They typically support real-time customer interaction and rely heavily on effective training and orientation. They may use expert systems to support training and just-in-time learning. Scripts for customer interaction (tacit knowledge made explicit) are also used.

At CIGNA *Property & Casualty,* for instance, management realized that a limited number of their own experts had an abundance of tacit knowledge that needed to be exploited and captured.

Identifying the high performers and knowledge gaps was the first step toward latent knowledge extraction. The next was to create a decision-support infrastructure that allowed knowledge to be provided to the rest of the organization. This knowledge needed to be translated from "many

the technology itself but from the new arrangements of organization, management, and people who can make the best use of it.

We'll outline these emerging roles and responsibilities in the next chapter, on Infrastructure. But we can't leave this chapter without discussing the changing role of the IT function and how to leverage the

to many" by: collecting insight, analyzing case summaries, segmenting cases by intent categories, identifying case patterns, and developing a case library with examples of best practice by category.

During the second stage, CIGNA developed an Underwriting Decision Summary model. The model allows employees to share their insights and create information.

Problem Resolution Systems. **Problem resolution systems apply "case-based reasoning" technology to the resolution of customer and other types of problems faced by an organization. This type of system uses knowledge that is structured into "cases" and probable scenarios. The benefits here are faster resolution, fewer expert personnel, and fewer hand-offs for problem resolution.**

Typical applications are the IT customer support systems offered by Hewlett-Packard, Compaq, Inference, and other computer product companies. These systems provide real-time information and problem-resolution support on products, pricing, and customer questions and problems.

Data-to-Knowledge Conversion Systems. **These systems rely on neural networks or other statistically oriented intelligent algorithms. They are usually combined with data visualization tools. However, it requires a smart person to know where to look and to generate hypotheses. This system is very popular with marketing groups. Data-to-knowledge conversion systems can include:**

- **Data mining—used in the analysis of large transaction-based databases in order to obtain customer purchasing behavior and demographics, which in turn are used to target markets with the right promotions and products.**
- **Decision support for knowledge work—used sometimes for underwriting and risk analysis.**
- **Real-time intelligent data analysis—systems that recalibrate waiting times, purchasing patterns, etc.**

knowledge of technologists and KM practitioners within the organization.

Participants in our studies report that they are drawing heavily on information technology departments to support their transfer effort; even better, they tell us their information technology staff is readily responding. In fact, by all accounts, KM practitioners are partnering with IT colleagues to adapt the appropriate information technology solutions to fit their evolving needs.

In 59 percent of the cases APQC has studied, corporate IT (or IS—information systems) is actively partnering with the knowledge management initiatives. And a full 35 percent of IT professionals have already been trained in knowledge management and best practice transfer concepts. "Only through symbiotic interaction between people and information technology can we truly gain competitive advantage in today's global economy," says Bipin Junnarkar of Monsanto.

This reality has not escaped the notice of KM pioneers:

At *Sequent*, KM and information technology organizations are functionally separate but work closely together. The CKO and CIO are peer positions in the organization. The information technology organization provides technology and human resources to support knowledge management programs and maintains the knowledge management information technology infrastructure. Whereas the CKO formulates KM strategy, the CIO and the information systems (IS) organization are responsible for defining information technology standards for the organization. The CKO and CIO jointly chair a corporate-wide steering committee to ensure that the common infrastructure is used, and used properly, by SCEL and other projects.

At *CIGNA*, technology is a critical component in learning and knowledge building. In developing an information technology structure, the IS team worked closely with the reengineering team to determine how information technology can best support the evolving needs.

At the *World Bank*, the Information and Technology Services Department is charged with supporting the knowledge management system with the appropriate technology, ensuring that the knowledge management system is fully integrated with other information systems.

At *National Semiconductor*, knowledge management initiatives are supported by corporate IS and engineering IT. There are fifteen to twenty-five individuals in engineering dedicated to defining standards, architecture, and tools for the engineering community. Corporate IS sustains a knowledge management/information access group of about ten individuals responsible for maintaining the data warehouse for corporate, sales/marketing, and manufacturing. Desktop integration is an additional responsibility of the corporate IS group.

Buckman reorganized to optimize knowledge sharing by creating a Knowledge Transfer Department (KTD) in March 1992. The KTD consolidated the IS and telecommunications departments and merged with the technical information center. Its mission is to plan, organize, and manage information system applications, infrastructure, and associated resources for rapidly disseminating collective industry, technical, and market knowledge that Buckman needs to gain a global competitive advantage.

CONCLUSION AND DESIGN LESSONS

Technology can be a powerful enabler of transfer effort. It can link people across time and space. It can spread knowledge and practices rapidly, efficiently, and cheaply throughout your organization. It can help document and capture formerly tacit knowledge. There is no doubt that behind the current popularity of KM is the potent combination of newly pervasive technologies and companies' realization that knowledge assets must be managed.

But while new technologies are making the transfer of practices and knowledge more affordable then ever before, companies that think that simply by developing an intranet they will make sharing happen are dangerously wrong.

There are both IT challenges (which platform, application, and tools to use and how to use them) and more important, supportive infrastructure issues (if you build it, will they come?) that companies must keep in mind when designing their KM/IT architecture.

Here, in a nutshell (it was a *big* nut, we know . . .) are the lessons gleaned from our experience and that of participants in our KMIT study that can help you take the first step, the right way.

Establish standards; they are the key to sustainability. Beware of the IT hodgepodge. If you are using technology to support your transfer effort, choose a standardized platform at the start. Be it an intranet or Lotus Notes setup, or perhaps a combination thereof, by designing an expandable system from day one, you ensure the future of the transfer effort. The benefits are twofold. First, investment in IT will not become obsolete. Second, by standardizing the core, firms can allow diverse parts of the organization to participate actively in developing new applications while ensuring that every new venture is compatible with its predecessors. Such careful attention prevents the formation of archipelagoes of knowledge, islands of expertise no one can reach without a boat.

Match the KM system with the KM objectives. There is no single right way to design a technology architecture to support knowledge transfer. By and large, the more tacit and high-value knowledge transfers often involve pointer systems or help desks manned by experts. A loose interchange and brainstorming session in the conference room with cookies may be more productive than using groupware. Hypermail can help you track and "remember" important spontaneous discussions. Simply throwing the latest and greatest at your employees will not make the share. So figure out what you want to share, how often and for what reason, and then build an IT solution that makes it happen.

Create a structure for classifying knowledge. Many companies reported that they could not organize their knowledge nor provide sufficient, IT-enabled access to it without an underlying structure or taxonomy. The structure specifies the categories and terms for the knowledge in which the firm is interested. It lets knowledge contributors classify their contributions, and later allows those searching for knowledge to find it easily. Other terms used to describe such a structure include "metadata" (data about data), a "content classification scheme," and "knowledge models." Some firms included the classification of knowledge contributions as a part of their design guidelines for knowledge contributions. Several firms also found it helpful to create a thesaurus for knowledge relevant to the organization. A thesaurus allows searchers to find the knowledge they seek even when it is classified under terms with which they are not familiar.

Heavily market your transfer applications and ensure they meet users' needs. "If we build it, they will come" works only with substantial attention to marketing. Several firms also stated that knowledge system designers must understand the daily behaviors of their customers; if there isn't an easy answer to the question "How will this improve my day?" the system will not be used. Some companies pointed out that knowledge managers should constantly publicize examples of successful use—another form of marketing. One noted that it was important in marketing the knowledge capability to use the language of the user—local terminology such as "best practices," "reuse," "cycle-time reduction," or "access to expertise," rather than the jargon of the knowledge management movement. "If they understand it, they will come" is probably a very true statement.

Remain flexible; nothing is etched in stone. Any particular knowledge management system or approach must be treated as provisional and temporary. Both knowledge and the technology for managing it change rapidly. Most firms started their knowledge management initiatives with pilot programs to learn how best to approach the problem. But others argued that the pilot stage is permanent: "All programs are provisional, all technologies subject to abandonment." One company felt that current IT tools are particularly immature and thus require "careful planning and trade-offs to deliver functional, well-performing solutions." Several firms emphasized flexibility in building and maintaining technology platforms. The key is to understand how customers are using the technology and respond rapidly with appropriate changes.

Maintain a pragmatic vs. perfectionist approach. One firm's byword was literally "Focus on what works, not perfection." Another company maintained that the right design for a knowledge management system will only be determined over time through customer behavior. Practicality was emphasized for knowledge structures, desired behaviors, and technology. One firm recommended that knowledge systems should be as easy to use as possible because a switch to a knowledge orientation is difficult enough without complex technologies.

Keep people first; KM is inherently people-based. Or, as one conceptually minded firm put it, KM is "fundamentally sociocultural." Because knowledge can only be surrendered voluntarily, many firms emphasized the importance of viewing knowledge management in human terms. Get as many people participating as possible. View every employee as both a content provider and a consumer. Use people, not just technology, in support roles for knowledge management. Some suggested emphasizing natural work groups and existing "communities of practice" rather than trying to create new ones. The strongest advocates of this lesson argued that best practice came from "focusing more on people and less on IT."

Measure the Impact of Knowledge Management. Because someone will ultimately question whether benefit is being derived from spending on knowledge management, many KMIT participants suggested that value and impact should be monitored from the beginning. One firm argued for close ties to the firm's measurement systems. Others advocated more anecdotal means of value measurement: "Collect anecdotal examples and testimonials of the contribution of knowledge management to the business result." Measuring and managing impact is difficult, and not all firms in the study do it. But many of those that do not measure and manage the impacts have nagging doubts that someday the proof of value will be required.

Chapter 11

CREATING THE KNOWLEDGE INFRASTRUCTURE

Even if you announce full senior management support for a best practices and knowledge transfer initiative; even if you put in the most sophisticated "anywhere-anytime-anybody" technology for sharing; and even if you provide incentives for sharing (recognition, promotion, money), you may get lousy results.

Why?

Because people need help in understanding and transferring best practices.

Almost every successful organization we have worked with realizes the need and importance of an explicit and institutionalized organizational infrastructure to assist the transfer of knowledge and best practices. (*How* they do it varies. *Who* does it varies. *What* they do varies. But *not* whether they do it.) These early practitioners know that transfer would never happen without a process, and an infrastructure of people dedicated to facilitating the process.

WHAT'S A KNOWLEDGE INFRASTRUCTURE ANYWAY?

Infrastructure includes the *transfer-specific mechanisms* put in place to ensure best practices flow throughout the enterprise. These include technology, work processes, and networks of people. *Infrastructure* also includes the organizational structure surrounding the processes: the essential line and staff roles that must be played to support the new initiative of knowledge transfer. That organizational structure has at least two layers.

Layer 1 is the micro structure. In the trenches are the "unsung heroes" of transfer; the people in nooks and crannies of the organization. We call them knowledge brokers, facilitators, librarians, and a hundred other new and old names. But whatever their title, we mean the people who are organized into roles, systems, and structures to make transfer happen.

Layer 2, the super structure, is the link to the formal organization structure. At some companies, the KM staff reports to a senior level of KM executives—be they CKOs, CIO, or director of quality knowledge networks (more on that later in this chapter).

Finally, *infrastructure* includes the cross-functional management processes that incorporate KM into the fabric of the organization: budgeting (who's gonna pay for this stuff?) and implementation (who "owns" it and is accountable for results?).

We find the most reliable test of the seriousness and effectiveness of a company's best practice transfer is whether or not it has put in place an explicit, supportive infrastructure that makes knowledge sharing a primary focus of someone. If no one is "charged" with watching out for transfer, it will fizzle and fade.

DON'T LEAVE CHANGE TO CHANCE

Like a lot of other things in life, transfer of knowledge and best practices doesn't just happen because it makes good sense. Or because management says it ought to. Building the right infrastructure to facilitate change is critical to ensuring the success of your transfer projects.

Change isn't automatic, or easy, or quick. We've mentioned some of the barriers to change in earlier sections, but as a reminder, there are six barriers that specifically hinder the transfer of know-how and practices, and which reinforce the need for an explicit knowledge infrastructure:

1. *Hidden knowledge*. People don't know what it is that they know, or that someone else needs it. They're sitting on a potential gold mine but don't realize it. They can't transfer something they don't know they have.
2. *Blindness*. Knowledge and best practices may exist (even down the hall), but the potential recipients don't know about it. They may suspect it exists but don't know how to find it. They don't search or don't know how to search. In effect, they are blind.

3. *Locked-up tacit knowledge.* Tacit knowledge—the know-how and judgment that come from experience, intuition, tricks, rules of thumb—is often 80 percent of the valuable knowledge in a process. But because such tacit knowledge is typically very hard to express and difficult to codify, the really valuable stuff remains "between the ears and behind the eyes" of the source. The recipient gets only the explicit (20 percent) portion of the valuable knowledge, and then wonders why the transplant failed.
4. *"We're different"* blinders. Potentially valuable knowledge and practices often don't transfer across functions, companies, industries—even entire sectors like education—because potential recipients focus on differences, not similarities of processes. They reject valuable knowledge due to parochialism, tunnel vision, ego, ignorance, protectionism, arrogance.
5. *"Sorry—I'm too busy."* Even if the transfer would save them time, they don't have time to save time. The transfer never gets a hearing.
6. *Implementation is hard.* Even if all of the previous barriers are overcome, the *transfer* of knowledge occurs, but action doesn't follow. It remains under construction or simply dies, for a variety of reasons—no money, fear of change, lack of leadership, no buy-in, turnover, no support, lack of training, change of management . . . you name it.

Unsuccessful organizations ignore these barriers and keep relying on the false assumption that just because best practices exist, Economics 101 predicts they will automatically transfer. They don't. Or if they do, it is only after a long lag and probably a slip in competitive rank.

How long?

Research by professors at Vanderbilt University showed that innovations in education have taken twenty-six years on average to move from the first 10 percent of early adopters to widespread acceptance. *That's long.* Unfortunate in education, but disastrous in industries where the rate of change is measured in nanoseconds.

THE BRAVE NEW WORLD OF CHANGE AGENTS

Successful organizations *don't* leave change to chance. They assign specific roles and responsibilities, and in some cases invent a nomenclature to describe these new roles. Some "titles" are borrowed from useful metaphors, such as the publishing industry or sports. Some organizations, such as Chevron and Hewlett-Packard, designate "process masters" or "internal consultants" who have specific process expertise in addition to facilitation expertise. Some companies centralize the transfer-related work under one head—the chief knowledge officer, or director of knowledge networks. At other organizations, KM "middle managers" report to business unit heads, the CIO, or the CEO.

Regardless of the reporting structure, these individuals, operating at the front lines of the best practice transfer movement, are charged with providing daily assistance, encouragement, and involvement to employees throughout the firm. Their job is to facilitate the flow of know-how and best practice, add value, edit, search, filter, and sort out.

THREE APPROACHES TO INFRASTRUCTURE

As we roam the world of transfer practitioners, we've run into all manner of enabling infrastructures. They range from low to high tech, from a few people to several hundreds. Regardless of the model's size and complexity, these infrastructures share some basic processes and fall into three general design approaches:

1. Self-directed
2. Knowledge services and networks
3. Facilitated transfer

The three are not mutually exclusive. In fact, they coexist in many organizations. The more advanced a company's KM practice, the greater

EMERGING KM TITLES

Knowledge management champion(s)	**Process masters**
Knowledge management managers	**Progress directors**
Publishers and publishing coordinators	**Progress consultants**
Librarians and information specialists	**Internal consultants**
Network or team leaders, and section managers	**Coordinators**
Help desk (content and process)	**Knowledge brokers**
Facilitators	**Cross-pollinators**
Shepherds	**Lightning rods**
Coaches	

FIGURE 11.1

Three Approaches to Infrastructure

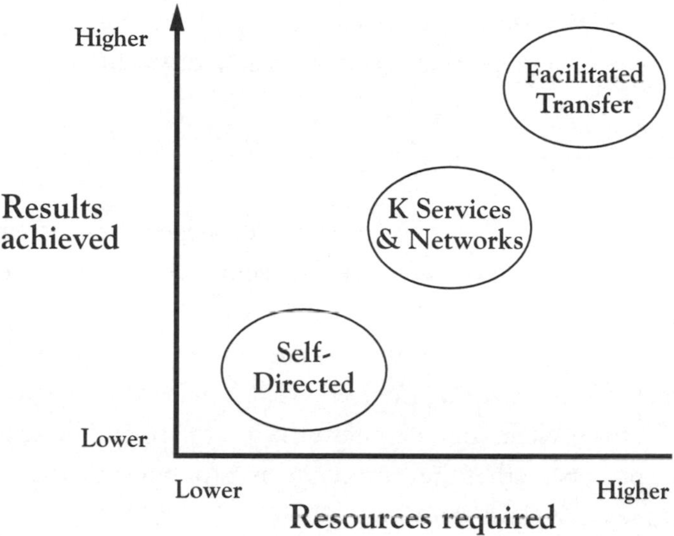

the likelihood that its transfer infrastructure will be rich in texture and multidimensional in design.

These three approaches can be placed on a continuum of ever-increasing likelihood of results and higher resources/commitment (see Figure 11.1). In Table 11.1, we've put some descriptive words that explain the characteristics and methods or each approach.

TABLE 11.1

How the Three Approaches Address the Barriers to Transfer

	APPROACHES		
Six Barriers	Self-Directed	Knowledge Services & Networks	Facilitated Transfer
1. Don't know		♌	♌
2. Blindness	♌	♌	♌
3. Tacit knowledge		♌	♌
4. We're different		♌	♌
5. Too busy			♌
6. Implementation			♌

APPROACH #1: SELF-DIRECTED

> *Descriptive words:* storage, codification, repository, database, retrieval, navigation, pointers, yellow pages, dissemination, intranets, Internet.

The *self-directed* approach to designing a knowledge infrastructure essentially says, "Here it is, now go use the technology to help you find what you want."

The self-directed approach is often augmented with "pointer systems" which can be anything from knowledge maps to corporate yellow pages. These systems don't contain the information or description of the best practice; rather they direct the user to someone who might know more about a particular topic.

The *database* is the key component. Companies that rely on this approach employ databases, repositories, autonomous agents, and search methodologies to allow employees easy access to the knowledge they require. Some electronic repository or knowledge base is the building block for all three design approaches, but in this case *it's the cornerstone*.

The knowledge base's main function is to capture data and information. It collects information from newspapers, journals, analysts' reports, other databases, field reports, the Internet, presentations, and the like, and stores them either as full text or abstracts. Think of these databases as electronic libraries and card catalogs. You can go there to look things up.

Texas Instruments calls this component of its KnowledgeBase the "Document Database." Sequent Computer employs two librarians to constantly record and access knowledge. Some companies even capture best practices tales in these knowledge bases. Both TI and Chevron have a best practices database where description of practices and results are electronically stored for later browsing.

Whatever their "name," these databases alone typically do little to transform the information into knowledge beyond some low-level purging and pruning; there is often no attempt to integrate the information into "valued oriented" packages tailored for use by the organization, or, as some firms call it, "making sense" out of information. That's up to each and every user to figure out.

Essentially, these databases *passively disseminate*; users "pull down" information they need, when they need it. Some databases provide value-added or somewhat-intelligent software (e.g., grapeVINE, Hoovers, or Excalibur) that serve as "autonomous agents." Agents kick out information to the user in accordance with a preset "interest profile" provided by the user.

Locator systems are the second main feature of this design approach. These are often called *pointers* or *maps* and tell users where to find particular information. Paraphrasing Samuel Johnson, the writer and philosopher, "The next best thing to knowing something is knowing where to find it." These maps range from simple directories supplying names, phone numbers, faxes, and e-mail addresses to search engines with taxonomic or full text research.

Most maps are electronic, but some companies, like Chevron, actually started with a paper version that folds just like a highway map. Chevron's map includes names, location, phone numbers, and other pertinent information for people in Chevron worldwide who are working in specified knowledge arenas. Hughes Space calls their locator the "*Knowledge Highway*." AT&T relies on an on-line directory of expertise. Coopers & Lybrand employees can call 1–800-KNOW-HOW to access a help desk with a human researcher who uses a database to locate expertise.

The self-directed approach is certainly useful. It helps users find information directly or to find a person who has the information they require. Thus, it partially addresses the "search" problem listed as one of the six items that frustrate the flow and implementation of knowledge. However, if falls short on addressing some of the other "barriers."

- A database really can't represent the treasure chest of "tacit knowledge" which may hold the greatest potential for improvement
- Even human pointer systems (à la Teltech—see below) are limited in that they rely on the users to initiate the quest and incorporate the findings
- It does little to overcome the internal cultural barriers of "we're different" and "we're too busy"
- It does nothing about moving to action

Ultimately, self-directed is a useful, but not sufficiently comprehensive, approach.

TELTECH'S LOCATOR SYSTEM

In 1984, Joseph Shuster leveraged his knowledge of how technical professionals work into a one-stop knowledge shop: The Teltech Resources Network Corp. The Minneapolis-based firm is a sort of a KM hybrid which allows its clients to access a plethora of "knowledge sources," from human experts (over 3,000 of them) to article clippings. Teltech "gatekeepers" help knowledge seekers find experts with knowledge on their topic of interest. This blend of human expertise (and "human search engines") and technological savvy allows Teltech clients to dramatically reduce the time it takes them to locate relevant experts.

The network has been so successful that Teltech has managed to embed its growing base of knowledge about locator systems into a new service; it now helps others set up their own locator systems. Says CEO Andy Michuda: "A couple of years ago, all the leading examples of KM revolved around Notes and intranet application; more recently, people have began to recognize that the people/expert component is the key."

Michuda recalls a recent client—a semiconductor maker—that has been laboring for years to "convert" all of its existing tacit knowledge into explicit form. The result: a very long process and a high level of frustration, not to mention a reservoir of mostly outdated information. Teltech helped the semiconductor company design a "low-tech" expert locator system instead. "The system offers navigational capabilities to access current, live, relevant knowledge," says Michuda, "in less time, with less money, and with a higher payback."

APPROACH #2: KNOWLEDGE SERVICES AND NETWORKS

Descriptive words: information services, help desk, networks, discussion databases, communities of practice, knowledge managers, knowledge integrators, knowledge packagers, want ads.

The second approach to designing knowledge infrastructures, *knowledge services and networks* goes further. In addition to providing self-directed components, this approach also provides a variety of knowledge management services and organized networks to assist in the transfer process. *Knowledge managers* and *knowledge integrators* add value by scanning the flow of information, and organizing or "packaging" knowledge into a more digestible and applicable format.

This approach also involves extensive networks of people who come together to share and learn from one another face-to-face and electronically (sometimes known as communities of practice—at one consulting firm, a network was four hundred members strong).

Given that knowledge is the principal product of consulting firms, it is not surprising firms such as Arthur Andersen, Ernst & Young, Price Waterhouse, Coopers & Lybrand, and McKinsey have major investments in infrastructure and employ this approach. But services and networks are also prevalent among many nonconsulting outfits as well, including Amoco, Buckman Labs, Chevron, the National Security Agency, and Texas Instruments.

This second approach not only involves sophisticated databases, but establishes the services and networks to leverage the collective experiences, skills, and intelligence of the organization.

ERNST & YOUNG

Like its Big Four consulting firm brethren (we offered examples from Arthur Andersen earlier in this book), Ernst & Young has made a significant investment in this KM infrastructure.

The firm's internal research found that up to 80 percent of its resident knowledge is not being applied to business processes in a systematic manner. Armed with the valuable knowledge of just how much it did not know, E&Y quickly adopted an extensive "Global Knowledge Sharing" approach; the infrastructure includes:

- Global Knowledge Steering Committee—with chief knowledge officers (CKOs) from key countries
- Global Knowledge Council—addresses specific functional strategy issues

- Five Centers for Business Knowledge which house the support staff for their initiatives
- One hundred Knowledge Networks—practice professionals responsible for collecting, storing, updating, and advancing the knowledge of the firm
- PowerPacks—a database for each E&Y Knowledge Network to store its reusable information
- EY/KnowledgeWeb—collective catalogued information available to all—200,000 accesses per month
- Knowledge Services Group, with three processes
  —Quick Response: fifteen information professionals who respond to inquiries, with a goal of responding within two hours: About 50 percent of the requests are for information for proposals; 25 percent want info for client service, and 25 percent relate to firm strategic planning issues
  —Research Group: handles in-depth inquiries where time and resources are required
  —Business Analysis Group: analyses of competitors

E&Y has many other specialized knowledge services, databases, and networks, all with the emphasis not on technology but on building a sharing infrastructure that everyone in the organization understands, and which "includes process owners, executive steering committees, and knowledge creators and integrators," according to John Peetz, chief knowledge officer.

BUCKMAN LABORATORIES.

It is hard to understand the depth of Bob Buckman's commitment to knowledge management and transfer until you've seen the laptops at each desk and workstation at his offices, listened to his commitment and conviction in one of his many presentations, seen his electronic network in action, and watched him participating in public meetings and pecking away on his own laptop.

A clear indication of Buckman's belief in the importance of transfer was the 1992 creation of the Knowledge Transfer Department, which he charged with:

- Accelerating the accumulating and dissemination of knowledge within the company
- Providing easy and rapid access to the company's global knowledge bases
- Teaching how to share best practices to all Buckman affiliates

The dedicated people who fill these roles complement an extensive technological "pull" system called K'Netix (see case study in Chapter 14, page 144) as well as transfer-targeted recognition and rewards. The "full service" approach has been paying off handsomely for Buckman. Indeed, the company credits much of their 250 percent growth in sales in the past decade to its system. Costs are down. Speed of response to customers is hours, not weeks or days, and quality of response has risen all over the world.

SEQUENT COMPUTER SYSTEMS

"We absolutely live or die by the knowledge of our people," says John McAdam, president and CEO of Sequent. His belief runs through the company's knowledge systems and underlies the design of Sequent's knowledge infrastructure.

For example, Sequent calls employees who produce knowledge "publishers," and employees who use it "consumers." To know what consumers want and need, the designers of the system brought together groups of "influencers" from across the company to find out what kinds of information was required and in what shape and form.

They found out that Sequent people wanted things they couldn't get elsewhere, such as outstanding presentations, scripts for sales calls, and design documents. They also found out that some people wanted information organized around the value chain, while others wanted a functional view. Rather than forcing them to choose one or the other, they do both; users of the Sequent Corporate Electronic Library can click on a "value chain" view button or an "organization" view button. To add value to knowledge transfer, change agents "listen in" on e-mail conversations and pull out the "threads" from the conversations and post them for later referral.

The knowledge services and networks approach addresses many of the transfer problems:

- It helps the organization "know more about what it knows."
- It facilitates "seeing" with databases and sophisticated search engines.
- It taps into tacit knowledge by stressing personal relationships.
- It helps people overcome the "we're different" block by using a process focus that looks beyond one's own functional silo, or firm, or sector; and adds incentives based on sharing, such as performance appraisals and recognition systems.
- It reduces the "we're busy" argument by providing helpful services.

The major difference between this approach and the "next level up" is that this approach to infrastructure does not necessarily include a trained cadre of facilitators and change agents dedicated to action and stationed throughout the organization.

APPROACH #3: FACILITATED TRANSFER

> *Descriptive words:* Facilitators, change agents, implementers, projects, technical assistance, consultants, guidance counselors, support personnel, brokers, coaches, shepherds.

The third approach to a knowledge transfer infrastructure is the "full service level." We call it "Facilitated Transfer," and it provides all of the previous activities and services, plus more.

This approach designates specific persons—full or part time—to stimulate, assist, and encourage transfer of knowledge and best practices; some even help with implementation. These change agents go by all sorts of names, from facilitators to progress directors. We've met brokers and cross-pollinators, not to mention boundary spanners, lightning rods, and champions.

Companies that opt for this full-service level assign specific transfer and facilitation responsibilities to full or part-time employees in plants and offices throughout an organization. These change agents are trained to assist other employees in:

1. Finding, capturing, codifying, and transmitting knowledge and best practices to the knowledge base
2. Helping fellow employees to solve problems and improve processes by helping them to use the databases and other knowledge services of their organization
3. In some cases, acting as internal consultants to facilitate implementation

This approach not only informs and enables transfer, it provides direct facilitation and help in the field for process improvement. The focus is on *implementation*.

Organizations taking the facilitated approach search for their facilitators from a cadre of people already in the organization. Some of the sources are:

- Internal "change agents" or consultants
- Team leaders and facilitators
- Trainers
- Benchmarking facilitators

AMOCO CORP.

Amoco began its "Shared Learning" program by assembling a group of people recruited from across the company, selected for their interest in organizational learning. This first group has now been expanded at every Amoco business unit where dedicated "change agents," called quality/progress professionals, are charged with helping employees make Shared Learning work.

Progress professionals coach fellow employees in process improvement techniques and how to participate in building the database; they provide training and spread the word, answer questions, and make sure all Amoco employees have access to tools. In addition, Amoco has "Networks of Excellence" made up of individuals who share a common business-related interest, and who meet regularly to discuss how they are facing challenges.

Amoco's Shared Learning network includes a three-tiered database structure. But Amoco is quick to point out that Shared Learning is not so much about databases as establishing networks of people who share knowledge. "Connecting those who have with those who need" is a favorite quotation from Dave Ledet.

Does all this work?

Attend any of their "ShareFairs" where employees get together to celebrate success, recognize each other, and exchange lessons learned. We *guarantee* it will make a believer of you. Or else sit in on their regular "Lunch and Learn" meetings in small groups across the company and feel and hear the enthusiasm and commitment.

TEXAS INSTRUMENTS

TI's late chairman Jerry Junkins established an Office of Best Practices to provide an ongoing infrastructure/mechanism to facilitate transfer. The vision was to move from an environment of "I have to solve my own problems" to one of looking for existing solutions not only from across TI, but also from benchmarking best practices in other businesses and sectors.

When TI first embarked on the development of the Best Practice Sharing project, like any pioneer, it knew very little about knowledge management and transfer and collaborative architectures. But through experience, TI quickly realized that simply creating a database of knowledge and best practices, publishing knowledge and best practices in memos or booklets, and attendance at conferences or seminars, would not necessarily—or even often—lead to action. TI decided it needed to create a mechanism for people-to-people, face-to-face transfers instead. Hence, as part of the structure of the Office of Best Practices, TI established a "facilitator network," headed by Cindy Johnson.

TI's best practice sharing team initially selected 138 "facilitators" worldwide; eventually their ranks swelled to over 200. These facilitators are TI employees who are improvement-minded, who naturally "trade" and "broker" knowledge, who are trusted by their colleagues, and who are good communicators. They are "pollinators" that make connections. And the more the better, for according to the "Law of the Telecoms," the value of a network is directly proportional to the square of the number of users.

The typical facilitator profile is:

- A leader; a source people often turn to for help; a team builder
- Interpersonal skills—ability to network well with people
- Knowledgeable about the benchmarking process
- Flexible; has a tolerance for ambiguity
- Comfortable with technology
- Some training and consulting skills

Each facilitator is given training in skills such as interviewing, root cause analysis, categorizing and documenting, and information searching. In addition, they learn how to access in-house and external electronic resources. Facilitators also rely on their own network for assistance in finding critical knowledge, and attend a quarterly one-day forum where they network with other facilitators, share success stories, and receive advanced training.

Facilitators can be found at every site and every business. Their role as facilitators is part-time only, ranging from 10 to 25 percent of their time. They still have "normal" jobs and report to their line or staff managers, and they get no extra compensation for being a facilitator. Rather, they are charged with the following missions:

- Collect best practices in their own area of activities
- Translate these into usable/transferable information
- Assign appropriate keywords (categories, topics, processes, etc.)
- Champion and publicize best practice sharing efforts
- Access the "KnowledgeBase" (TI's best practices database) for solutions to problems
- Ask questions, see patterns, link practices back to business problems
- Show others how to access best practices information; identify people they may wish to talk to or visit
- Assist in implementation of the practices if asked to do so

WHERE DO FACILITATORS COME FROM?

One great source of potential change agents is the quality improvement (TQM) department or some other internal consulting organization. Such central groups support and coordinate a network of internal "change agents" or consultants, usually with representatives in each of the units. Amoco has one. TI has one. Chevron and Citibank each boast an internal consulting office, as do many others. This central "node" or corporate hub of the "improvement network" is typically quite small and performs many roles including:

- Maintaining the corporation's common language and framework for change and improvement (for example, "TI-Best"; "The Chevron Way"; Amoco's "Shared Learning" and Amoco Business Model; Motorola's Six Sigma)
- Providing central information technology architecture for best practices and other databases (the "best practices" database usually resides here)
- Conducting internal quality assessments using the Malcolm Baldrige National Quality Award criteria or a customized version of it
- Providing training, professional development, and support for the facilitators, coordinators, and changes agents out in the business units
- Providing access to external resources
- Educating senior executives on improvement initiatives
- Communicating the above to the entire organization (usually in conjunction with the internal communications function)
- Acting as a liaison with the training and communication organization

NEXT LEVEL: THE SUPERSTRUCTURE

At some companies, the three-dimensional design of the KM infrastructure is anchored by a "superstructure," a top-level KM champion with formal and enterprisewide responsibility for coordinating and directing the company's multiple transfer initiatives.

Such designated leaders and champions seem to be located both at the corporate and the business unit levels (see Figure 11.2). They are

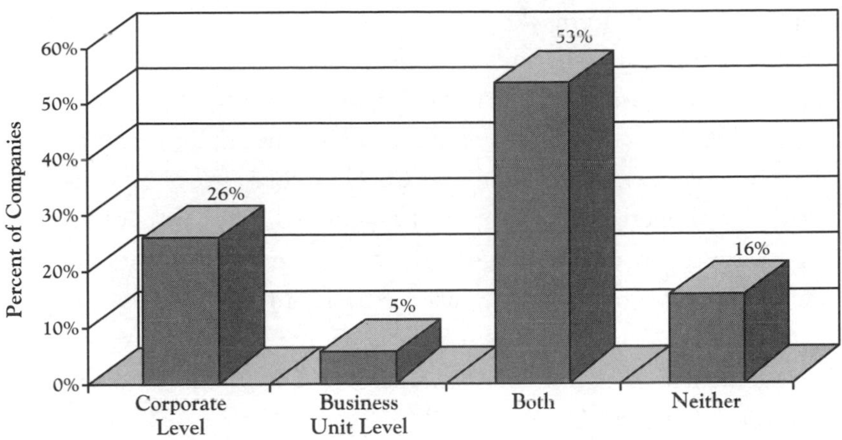

FIGURE 11.2
Knowledge Management Champion

partnering with their information technology colleagues to adapt the appropriate information technology solutions to fit the need.

Most recently, the business media pundits have given a lot of press to the creation of a few chief knowledge officers (CKO) and chief learning officers (CLO) in some major corporations, such as General Electric, Coca-Cola, and Monsanto.

At *Sequent Computer Systems*, the chief knowledge officer has a global, corporate responsibility for all knowledge management programs and infrastructure. The CKO and his team provide corporatewide infrastructure, corporatewide formal educational programs, various operational support and program management and coordination for knowledge management initiatives inside the company. The CKO is also responsible for the corporation's patent portfolio and for traditional corporate research services, such as the corporate library. Sequent's manager of corporate research services, who reports to the CKO, is responsible for the corporation's physical library and for SCEL, which is considered knowledge management infrastructure.

At *Coca-Cola*, CLO Judy Rosenblum manages groups of facilitators around the world who help identify and transfer successful practices. Rosenblum has a dual reporting relationship to the vice president of human resources and the CEO.

At *GE*, Steve Kerr serves as the CLO and vice president of leadership development. Kerr, who reports to the head of HR, says: "This is a terrific opportunity for human resource executives. Now they can apply their expertise to help the company get better at a major new thing." The new thing? Transfer of knowledge and best practices.

How does a CLO differ from a CKO? Their jobs are on a continuum, with a lot of overlap. If a company has adopted the mantra of becoming a learning organization, it's likely to appoint a CLO. If its rhetoric refers instead to leveraging knowledge as an intellectual asset, it may opt for a CKO. To send the message that shared learning or knowledge management is a high priority, the CLO or CKO reports to the top, most often to the CEO.

So far, the CKO and his or her namesakes are the exception, not the rule. But that does not mean companies are not serious about their KM work. Andy Michuda, CEO of Teltech, says his firm's research has found no correlation between the existence of a CKO (or equivalent) and the effectiveness of the KM projects. Indeed, he says, "some 45 percent of the companies we meet may not have a CKO, and they 'may not talk the talk' but they *walk the walk*; they may not have formal management positions but they've got this readiness and grass-roots effort." Teltech's research confirms ours: The real action in KM is not happening at the CKO level. And when the media choose to focus on fancy new titles they miss the main event: the grass-roots, organization-wide proliferation of KM practitioners, from editors to facilitators, who provide the real engine of knowledge.

WHICH APPROACH IS RIGHT FOR US?

First, understand that there isn't a single *right* approach. The three design approaches discussed here are more like steps leading to a "full-service" or multidimensional solution. Leading KM companies have elements of all three populating their infrastructure.

Second, critical infrastructure choices are (or should be) influenced by geography, culture, money, technology, leadership, market structure, philosophy—but most of all, by the answers to these three questions:

1. How important is transfer of knowledge and best practices in the strategy of the organization?

2. How much assistance and intervention does the organization think is required to make transfers happen and get results in their organization in a timely manner?
3. How does the infrastructure address the six problems with the flow of knowledge and its implementation?

We reiterate that the three approaches—self-directed, knowledge services and networks, and facilitated transfer—are not discrete. They depict a continuum, along which organizations choose the mix of activities. Which is better? Each organization has to balance the answers to these questions with their resources, their strategy, and their belief in the importance of knowledge and best practices transfers in the years ahead.

Chapter 12

MEASURING THE IMPACT OF TRANSFER

The fundamental building material of a modern corporation is knowledge. Using knowledge to make money is the real challenge.

—Valery Kanevsky, Hewlett-Packard Company

Some experts wax sentimental about the benefits of transferring and managing knowledge and the all-around warm and fuzzy feeling of sharing and learning. No argument here. We love sharing. And learning is great fun. But the business world is not (only) about having fun. Realists (and most managers are of that ilk) know that the key is figuring out how to better manage knowledge assets to maximize their returns.

It's as simple as that. And it's as complex as that.

"Maximizing returns" implies that we can: (1) measure the "principal" investment, and (2) measure the yield from that investment on some periodic basis. Both are debatable when it comes to putting figures on things as intangible and ephemeral as the value of knowledge and best practices sharing.

Debatable, perhaps. But not impossible!

And so, whereas measurement is the *least* developed area in the emerging knowledge management "discipline," we believe it to be critical, as well as an area where true leadership can make a real difference.

CLUES TO VALUE

Knowledge is beginning to be widely accepted as the atom-equivalent, basic ingredient of today's competitive advantage, and this presents KM practitioners with a true challenge. Like early quantum mechanics theorists, they *know* it is there but they cannot *see* it. "A scientist had to imagine uncountable corpuscles banging invisibly this way and that in the soft pressure of wind against his face," writes James Gleick, in *Genius*, his biography of physicist Richard Feynman. Like early physicists, exponents of KM must infer the existence of knowledge, assume its potential and powers by observing its impact on other forces, such as the forces of competition and innovation, stock market valuations, employee morale productivity, and product excellence. Here are three clues to potential "value" of knowledge within a corporation:

Clue #1: Stock Prices

The stock market routinely assigns higher valuations to "intelligent firms" versus ones with stockpiles of hard assets, like brick and mortar. The gap between the value of a firm's tangible assets and its market capitalization implies there's some other asset at work: namely, knowledge.

Sometimes, knowledge is the *only* asset. For an extreme manifestation of what knowledge can be worth, take the mid-1990s spate of successful "concept" IPOs (Initial Public Offerings). The Netscapes of this world. These are technology start-ups, which include a bunch of smart guys with a couple of great ideas. No revenues. Negative cash flow. Yet they command hefty dollar valuations from such savvy—and not uncynical—folks as venture capitalists and Wall Street bankers. What gives? What investors pay for is their assumption about the worth of the collective IQ of the new enterprise. Those who invested in Netscape have not been disappointed.

The same applies to more mature firms such as Coca-Cola, Microsoft, and Sun Microsystems. These companies routinely trade at many times their book value—and usually at higher multiples than industry peers. The gap between them and the next guy represents a *knowledge-based competitive advantage*. They take more intelligent action based on what they know—about markets, about products, and about customers. About how to share and innovate.

The combined experience and "capital" of the organization—some in the heads of workers, some in the brand loyalty of customers, and some embedded into the structure of the organization—represent a growing portion of what a company is worth. Often, the intellectual assets and knowledge capital of a company are worth *three or four times* its tangible book value!

When Apple Computer bought Next for $400 million, it did not buy plants or buildings, points out Knowledge Capital™ measurement expert Paul Strassmann, "It bought $400 million worth of knowledge."

Clue #2: Performance Improvement

Stock market valuations are good only up to a point. We all remember J. P. Morgan's famous adage: "The markets will fluctuate." And boy, do they. When the market loses 10 percent of its value on a day in early spring, do the underlying companies become instantly 10 percent less intelligent? When the Dow Jones technology index drops 150 points in an afternoon, does the collective IQ of these companies' employees suddenly plunge?

Obviously not.

But whereas market value proxies are beneficial (for starters, they tell you just how much the market is willing to pay for smarts) they are but a proxy for the *Real Thing*. The *real* potential returns on optimal utility of knowledge assets lie in corporate performance measured through a plethora of competitive, operational, process, and financial measures.

Companies that *know what they know* can make better decisions—*faster*. Those that have mastered their collective intelligence develop *better* products and have a chance at capturing new markets—first. Let us repeat these three mantras of modern-day competition: Faster! Better! First! "What used to take weeks now takes hours. What used to take months now takes a week," says Mark Koskiniemi, vice president of human resources at Buckman.

Clue #3: The Cost of Not Knowing = "CONK"

There are lots of examples where information and knowledge were somewhere in the organization, but not where they needed to be to avoid a disaster. When the *Challenger* space shuttle exploded, some engineers at NASA knew the O-rings wouldn't hold at low temperatures. But the people who made the decision to launch did not. A company may launch a new service in China, but if the new team can't build on past experience in that market, it will make all the same mistakes again. A new movie comes out and preview audiences hate it, but that information comes too late to fix it. Sometimes, the cost of not managing knowledge is easier to pinpoint than the positive contribution of effective management. Easier. But can you afford it?

MEASURE VS. NURTURE

It's not entirely surprising that measurement is the least developed aspect of knowledge management and best practice transfer efforts. In fact, many practitioners believe that trying to measure before you understand how knowledge gets created and shared may lead you to focus on the wrong things.

To date, there are two general schools of thought on measuring the transfer of knowledge and best practices.

The first school can be called the "Nurturers." Its adherents believe measurement of knowledge management and transfer efforts is currently premature. Proponents of this point of view hold that not enough is yet known about the dynamics and the impact of knowledge to justify elaborate measurement systems. Hence, measurement at this early juncture can be risky and misleading, and the results suspect.

The second school, the "Quantifiers," is suspicious of the first school, and believes that measurement is important, both for understanding and legitimizing investment. It wants to know where and how to invest.

We probably edge over slightly into the second school. We believe measurements are key to ensuring the sustainability and success of transfer efforts over time. Top management will not continue to invest if no tangible or quantifiable intangible results can be demonstrated. To keep transfer efforts going, and centered, companies must continuously link their process to the desired outcome—their original value proposition. Without that link, efforts will likely lose their direction and purpose.

Are we "quantifiers"? Not quite. In fact, we are quite sympathetic to the "nurturers." It may be more productive in the early stages of transfer efforts to measure in order to observe, monitor, and nurture. It may be better to celebrate successes, early and often, and only later work out elaborate schemes for measuring knowledge management. Many KM pioneers, like Sequent Computer Systems, believe that trying to measure before you understand how knowledge management is working in your organization may cause you to focus on, and reward, the wrong things. So understand first; measure second.

Ultimately, we believe everything depends on *what kind of measurements* you are talking about and for *what purpose*.

If you want to know whether transfer efforts are achieving their objectives, identify the business results that match your original value proposition and measure those.

If you want to know which of your transfer tools and applications are the most effective for the purpose of sharing practices and know-how, measure the level of transfer activity, and ask users how it has helped them achieve business objectives.

Finally, for a comprehensive view of your knowledge management activities: measure both!

A PRACTICAL APPROACH TO MEASUREMENT

Whereas there are evolving and highly sophisticated ways to measure knowledge that go beyond traditional accounting, we believe that currently the best way to measure the impact of knowledge and best practice transfer is not by gauging the size of your knowledge capital base, but rather the effect it has on your company's performance.

And we are not alone. Indeed, measuring the benefits and results of knowledge management per se does not seem to be prevalent in the firms we have studied, which includes most of the leaders in knowledge management (see Figure 12.1). Practitioners tell us it is *more* important to measure the success of the projects and business processes that are being improved through the transfer of knowledge and best practices. Hence they attempt to link the outcomes of these efforts to their

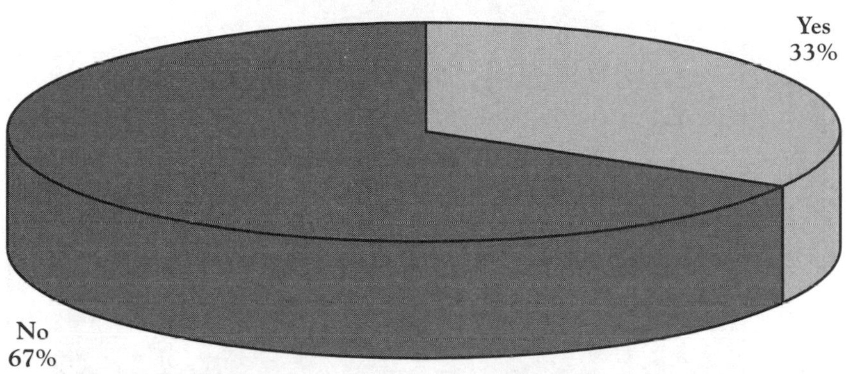

FIGURE 12.1
Companies with KM Measures of Effectiveness

original value proposition. Each comes with its own set of "process" and even financial measures. Hence we believe in measuring processes, activities, operational outcomes.

As any statistician will tell you, however, if transfer and sharing is made part of work, and performance improves, there are not enough regression analysis tools in existence to help you figure out the relative contribution of knowledge management versus other factors.

Although they may not be measuring the impact of their overall knowledge strategy, most firms are using some combination of yardsticks to gauge the success of their transfer projects. In fact, most can clearly describe process improvement outcomes in projects in which knowledge management approaches and applications were used. The most commonly mentioned improvement outcomes were improvements in process cycle time and quality of products, and business growth from the production and success rate of proposals and increased customer satisfaction (see Figure 12.2).

MEASURING THROUGH OUTCOMES

Since most of the companies with which we work report that their knowledge management efforts are tightly linked to business objectives and business needs, most prefer to measure *process and project outcomes*.

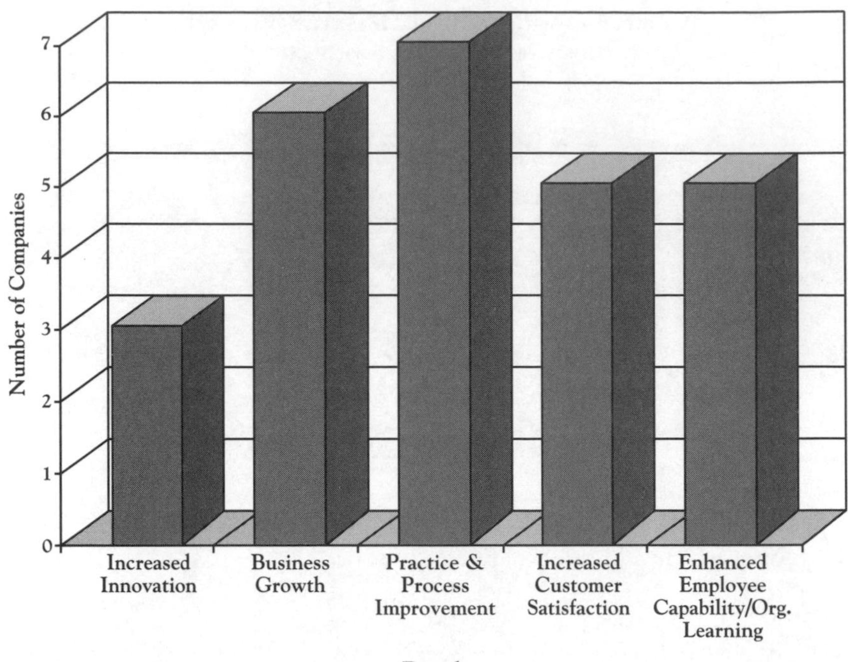

FIGURE 12.2

Outcomes Realized as a Result of KM Practice

For knowledge management applications to be perceived as successful by their users, they need to help users do their job or achieve an immediate business objective. Because this measurement is embedded in the business case scenario, the success of the project serves as a proxy for the success of the knowledge management application. In other words, knowledge management is seen as a tool for enhancing a business or improvement process.

Companies like Buckman and Sequent have implemented enterprisewide systems to support the sharing of knowledge and practices, especially in the sales and marketing arena. They focus on the impact on the value proposition, not the success of knowledge management individually.

Example 1: Sales from New Products.

A good example of measuring business results is Buckman's global measure of sales from new products. In March 1992, Buckman Labora-

TYING MEASURES TO THE VALUE PROPOSITION

When measuring the impact of transfer efforts, take into account your original goal. Each value proposition comes with a set of logical "measures" that help monitor your progress toward that goal, these could include:

Customer intimacy
- **Customer retention rates**
- **Number of calls handled per day**
- **Number of calls resolved on the first "sitting"**
- **Cross-selling penetration**
- **Increased revenue from existing customers**

Product leadership
- **Revenues from commercialization of new product**
- **Percentage of revenues from new products**
- **Time-to-market cycles**
- **Ratio of successful to unsuccessful product launches**
- **Number of launches per year**

Operational Excellence:
- **Cost per unit**
- **Productivity and yields**
- **Number of defects/poor quality**
- **Production cycle time**
- **Inventory carrying costs**
- **Environmental compliance**
- **Safety records**

tories International introduced K'Netix, a corporate-wide knowledge-sharing communication system. One of the value propositions behind K'Netix was improving product commercialization by linking sales people to customers and R&D. To measure how successful its efforts have been, Buckman examines percent of sales generated from new products (less than five years old). The results, which speak for themselves, are shown in Figure 12.3.

Buckman Laboratories International links this improvement partially to the KMIT efforts:

- The speed of response to customers is hours, not days or weeks.
- The quality of response has risen all over the world.

Percent of Sales from New Products	
1988–1992 (prior to K'Netix):	23.6%
1992–1996:	33.3%

FIGURE 12.3

- Office costs are down; the office is anywhere.
- Employee competency has increased, since more employees are immersed in high-intensity projects.
- The role of managers is not to manage the flow of information up and down the organization, but to close the gaps.

Ultimately, Buckman believes it impossible to put a monetary value on the knowledge network; it is fundamental to the way the company operates. Most of the companies we work with are highly sophisticated in the use of process, project, and enterprise-level measures. Many, such as CIGNA, use a balanced scorecard or family-of-measures approach.

Example 2: A Balanced Scorecard

The rationale behind the balanced scorecard (BSC) system was that learning was directly linked to process performance, which in turn affected corporate performance. At CIGNA Property & Casualty, the BSC is a means to measure and communicate with four aspects of the organization's effectiveness: financial, internal business, external business (customer), and learning and growth. To construct the model, CIGNA P&C needed to provide a set of corporate goals and direct performance measures as a framework.

To enhance the BSC results, CIGNA identified eight main competencies that needed improvement. These included the abilities to:

1. select and enter new markets with above-average profit potential
2. select and attract the right kinds of customers

3. select and manage the producers for those businesses
4. better identify exposures and hazards
5. drive pricing more accurately toward the right risk assessment
6. form partnerships with customers in order to reduce claims frequency
7. reduce claims severity
8. manage claims performance to the required service level of each business unit

CIGNA can now measure improvement by measuring change in each of the eight categories. Overall, CIGNA's consistently profitable results point to a dramatic turnaround, a result of improved decision making and faster work flow.

MEASURING THROUGH ACTIVITIES

Whereas management, customers, and employees care about how well the process is working and the results that are obtained, the architects of transfer initiatives must understand the activities behind the systems. Hence, this second group of measures indicates how frequently users are accessing, contributing to, or drawing on the information technology tools that enable transfer enterprise-wide.

Most of these measures reflect an Internet or Web browser paradigm, such as hits per page or submissions per employee. There is value in these activity measures. They can lead to a greater understanding how, or if, a tool or support system of the transfer activity is being utilized.

A caution: though activity-based measures provide useful information on accessibility, utilization, content quality, and design features, they do not provide information about the impact of these activities on results.

Common activity measures include:

- user rating of effectiveness
- number of hits
- participation rates
- frequency of contribution
- frequency of use

Arthur Andersen, for example, measures usage and user ratings of effectiveness and solicits user "success stories" such as faster report production (by using existing knowledge) to illustrate the success of its transfer systems. TI, like many other firms, counts the times employees log in to its best practice databases. Most recently, the hits rate was about 2,000,000 per month. Increases in hit rate indicate KM is penetrating the consciousness of a greater number of employees and becoming endemic to the way "work is done."

Ultimately, to gain a comprehensive view of transfer efforts success, firms rely on the combination package of outcomes and activity measures.

ACTUAL COSTS AND RETURNS

To add yet another level of "measurement," some firms track the actual cost of KM and transfer projects. Those are notoriously hard to pin down, because they are often dispersed throughout the organization, and can "hide" in places like IT, marketing, HR and training, as well as management time and the efforts of facilitators (see Chapter 11, which treats the knowledge infrastructure).

However, since there are costs associated with developing support systems, it helps to measure them. For example, at *Sequent*, the total spending on KM infrastructure (people and technology) is well under $1,000 per employee per year, including all direct costs and some portion of the indirect costs. *Buckman* spends about 3.75 percent of revenue on knowledge management and transfer activities, across the board. Hence, the all-inclusive cost per employee is about $7,500 per year for hardware, software, telephone, network, and staff support.

Obviously, the range is quite broad. And just because Sequent calculates a spending of $1,000 per employee does not mean its transfer efforts are less enthusiastic or successful (as their case study in Chapter 17, page 170, illustrates). The difference in per-employee charges reflect more accounting (what gets counted as KM-direct expense) than effort.

What Gets Counted?

Knowledge exchange and transfer applications (see Chapter 10 on using information technology) incur less up-front hardware and software cost to deploy (if you have the Intranet and/or Notes infrastructure already deployed), but keep in mind that they may require significant ongoing support costs to be successful.

These support costs include:

1. facilitating the formation and health of communities of practice and discussion groups
2. populating best practice databases
3. creating information technology standards for format and information and document management
4. advertising the existence of groups and experts
5. developing policies and procedures for appropriate use of information and dialogue

PERSPECTIVES ON MEASUREMENT

The bottom line is the bottom line. So if your company is doing much better, overall, just how concerned should you be about measuring the impact of transfer?

Very concerned.

Although measurement of the success of KM and transfer initiatives is perhaps the least developed area in this evolving field, it is a critical component of the creation an environment that both encourages and sustains sharing. Without *measurable success*, enthusiasm from employees and management will dissipate. And without *measurable success*, you won't be able to tell what works and what doesn't.

Just how to measure the impact of transfer is a subject of much debate. We applaud the efforts of "quantifiers" who have managed to calculate what knowledge is worth. But we recommend the use of practical process-outcome and activity measures, which, combined, give you a realistic assessment of "how you're doing."

Ultimately, knowledge about your knowledge management initiatives is important because it helps you:

- Design future systems and applications
- Improve the current sharing processes
- Ensure the transfer effort stays on track (that is, delivering the value proposition!)

As the role of knowledge managers within organizations grows, these measures will provide the underpinning of their performance evaluation and, hence, compensation.

If you cannot measure it, can you manage it? We don't think so.

Part Four

REPORTS FROM THE FRONT LINES

PIONEER CASE STUDIES

Some companies have successfully adopted internal transfer of knowledge and best practices as a competency and improvement strategy. They've stopped dreaming, debating, and discussing it. They are doing *it.*

From our work with over seventy organizations, we have chosen four to tell you about in detail in this section: Buckman Laboratories, Texas Instruments, the World Bank, and Sequent Computer Systems. We chose them as much for their differences as for their similarities. Their stories illustrate there is no "right" way to leverage knowledge. No "cookie cutter" design. No one-size-fits-all approach. Each of these four pioneers has chosen a different path to climb the mountain, but all four are setting their sights on the same peak.

What's it like up there?

For starters, it's getting crowded. While some companies attempt this journey with little idea of what awaits at the top, this part gives you an early and rare peek at the peak. The birds-eye view from the top. This is your chance to glimpse how effective management and transfer of knowledge has transformed four organizations. You can do it, too. We tell you more about how in Part Five.

Chapter 13

THE VIEW FROM THE TOP

Consider these sky-high achievements:

Privately held specialty chemical manufacturer Buckman Laboratories has retrained its global sales force and watched sales of new products climb.

How? By creating an electronic best-practice sharing engine that allows everyone to learn just enough, just in time. "Since it involves the entire company to get an improvement of this magnitude, and particularly on the interface with the customer, I believe that this is solid evidence of an ability to satisfy customers better and faster. In other words the productivity of the entire company went up," says CEO Bob Buckman.

Giant-size Texas Instruments has rediscovered growth and agility à la Silicon Valley startup.

How? By weaving a connective tissue of best practice sharing which has breathed new life into its reengineered, downsized corporate body. "We felt we need to find a new paradigm for reaching the next level of improvement," says Cindy Johnson, director of TI's Office of Best Practices. "We had to find ways to become more agile and learn faster so that we can innovate faster than our competitors."

The World Bank is redefining how developing nations attempt to resolve poverty and redress poor living conditions.

How? By pulling regional resources and specialist know-how and making it available to experts throughout the organization. They now know what works and what doesn't. They know what they know. "The Bank Group's relationships with governments and institutions all over the world and our unique reservoir of development experience across sectors and countries position us to play a leading role in [a] new knowledge partnership," said president James Wolfensohn. ". . . We need to become, in effect, the 'Knowledge Bank.'"

Mid-size Sequent Computer Systems has morphed itself into a big-time player in the high end of the UNIX market.

How? By leveraging internal knowledge and transferring best practice among its front-line employees. "With the kind of competition we have, we have to act and look bigger than we are, and the only way to do that is by sharing information," says Roger Swanson, manager of Corporate Research Services at Sequent.

ALL RIVERS LEAD TO THE SEA

Look once . . . These four organizations seem to have little in common.

But now, look again . . . While different in some ways, all four have adopted a methodical and strategic approach to the sharing of knowledge and best practices. They have defined the business objectives; sketched out a technology and organizational infrastructure; targeted the components of the knowledge-process (embodiment and dissemination) they seek to manage. They have begun to manage and measure the process of KM with a sensitivity to culture and an appreciation of the possible pitfalls.

Perhaps the most intriguing commonality among these four organizations is the emerging outward focus. As Peter Drucker once said, "The purpose of an organization resides outside the organization." While initially they focus on helping knowledge and best practices flow seamlessly in-house, they plan ultimately to open up their collective IQs to the browsing of external constituents.

Both Sequent and the World Bank recognize that distributors, alliance partners, regional banks, outsourcing services providers, vendors, suppliers, and customers will gain from gaining access to their knowledge bases. More to the point, they recognize they, too, stand to gain much by forming more intricate, knowledge-intensive ties with the external business environment. *This is not about selfless sharing. It's about sharing in order to win.*

And winning has never been tougher or more complex. As Brandeis professor Ben Gomes-Cassares explains in his book, the *Alliance Revolution*, today's competitive environment operates by new rules. "The entire nature of the competitive environment has changed," he says. "Markets are more fragmented. Economies of scale more difficult to achieve. Companies no longer compete one against the other. Rather, they do battle in 'constellations.'"

What holds these constellations together? What is their center of gravity?

They are held together by the binding ties of knowledge. Those companies that share more have longer-lasting, more intimate, more successful relationships with the planets around them, be they customers, suppliers, or partners.

A PASSION FOR KNOWING

Finally, there is one more reason we wanted to share these four stories with you. Their passion for knowing. At all four organizations, KM leaders speak with a contagious enthusiasm about their work. And it is that passion for knowledge and sharing which seems to permeate throughout the organization that makes Buckman, Sequent, the World Bank, and Texas Instruments ideal examples of knowledge in action.

You should be able to find yourself in one or all of them.

Chapter 14

BUCKMAN LABORATORIES

EMPOWERED BY K'NETIX®

An off-the-shelf CompuServe application is the neural knowledge network that energizes Buckman Laboratories. The Memphis-based Buckman aims to arm each associate, particularly front-line sales folks, with the collective IQ of the organization. And it relies on K'Netix , the Buckman knowledge network, to do the job. Launched in 1992, this electronic buffet of best practices, discussion forums and "just-in-time" training is credited with speeding up response time, increasing new product development, and boosting overall growth.

Psychologists often refer to it as the "Ah-ha!" moment; it is that split second of realization when an insight hits and irreversibly alters our paradigm of how the world works. For Buckman Laboratories, a specialty chemical company, the moment of enlightenment came in the late 1980s when Bob Buckman, chairman of BuLab Holdings, Inc., parent company of Buckman, was at home recuperating from a back injury. Two weeks in bed had rendered the energetic chairman utterly frustrated with his inability to "know" what was going on at work. He realized that others must be feeling similarly distressed by knowledge vacuums.

Necessity *is* the mother of invention.

Buckman began to envision a knowledge-driven company linked globally by an electronic network offering ready access to best practices, experiences, and skills to Buckman's 1,200 associates (employees) in eighty countries. Upon his return to the office, Buckman turned this bedridden fantasy into viable commercial reality—with stunning results.

> Since the 1992 introduction of K'Netix®, Buckman's KM and transfer of best practices system, new product-related revenues are up 10 percent and sales of new products are 50 percent higher. Response time to customer queries is down to hours, instead of days or weeks. "We have seen the payoff," says Mark Koskiniemi, Buckman's vice president of human resources.

BUCKMAN BEGAT KTD

Buckman's KM value proposition is providing associates at the point of customer contact with instantaneous access to the collective IQ of the organization. Thus armed, associates can make intelligent and immediate decisions that affect customer relations and—ultimately—revenue. "This [KM] system is dedicated to the front lines," says Bob Buckman. "It's a library of the important information relevant to the business of the customer."

Buckman's first structured effort to share and capture knowledge began in 1988 with the initiation of a *case history* system. This electronic best practice reservoir helps resolve customer problems faster and more efficiently by first applying existing "Buckman knowledge" about what works. By mid-1997, Buckman associates could access close to 2,500 customer case histories—1,787 in English and 685 in Spanish.

What did Buckman learn? That sometimes you need a KM-dedicated group to get the ball rolling.

In March of 1992, Buckman reorganized further to optimize knowledge sharing through the creation of a Knowledge Transfer Department (KTD). The KTD consolidated separate IS and telecommunications departments and merged with the technical information center. KTD's mission is to proactively respond to Buckman's global knowledge needs by planning and managing the resources necessary to rapidly disseminate collective industry, technical, and market knowledge to all associates. More specifically, KTD is charged with:

What did Buckman learn? That sometimes you need a KM-dedicated group to get the ball rolling.

- Accelerating the accumulation and dissemination of knowledge within the company
- Providing easy and rapid access to the company's global knowledge bases
- Sharing best practices with all Buckman associates

AND KTD BEGAT K'NETIX

If KTD is the corporate " nerve center," then the neural network it employs to speed knowledge throughout the corporate organism is K'Netix. Launched in 1992 using the CompuServe platform, K'Netix pulls together disparate technologies to allow twenty-four-hour, click-of-the-icon access from the desktop (or laptop) to associates worldwide. Users can dial in using a local CompuServe number, log onto the

ANATOMY OF A SYSTEM

K'Netix is Buckman's trademarked term for the way they use the Knowledge Sharing interface (K'Netix is not an application—it is a system of applications, much like an Apple "Launcher" or the Windows 95 "Start" menu). It functions like connecting tissue which brings together different programs and systems, some old, some new, some compatible and some not. It contains electronic forums, on-line libraries, a knowledge base, electronic mail, Internet/World Wide Web, intranet, project tracking systems, customer relationship management systems, groupware, bulletin boards, virtual conference rooms, and databases that capture institutional memory that is then made accessible to all employees. Access to K'Netix is available through the K'Netix Access Menu (KAM), which allows users to tap into the following components:

- ***BL Systems* contains component databases that relate to the business operations and systems such as accounting and order management.**
- **The *Buckman folder* contains an accumulation of technical knowledge to solve customer problems. Within this "folder" are forums that are the central point of the knowledge system—TechForum, ChemForum, EuroForum, AAAForum for Asia, Australia, and Africa, and ForoLatino. Each of these facilitates the communication of information throughout the organization worldwide. Because worldwide operations necessitate communication on various timelines, associates can communicate on-line, leave messages, and set appointments for real-**

Buckman server, and access everything from electronic forums to online libraries, electronic mail, the Internet/World Wide Web, project tracking systems, customer relationship management applications, bulletin boards, and virtual conference rooms. (See page 144.)

Technology purists may balk at this IT hodgepodge as well as at relying on an external vendor for both network backbone and some actual applications. It is certainly not "elegant," in IT terms, and proves a killer when it's time for an upgrade. But "piggybacking" off CompuServe's existing network infrastructure meant Buckman was ready to launch in only thirty days in 1992!

time interaction. The dialogue in forums proceeds without filtering, but the best threads are captured by technical experts and put in the library.

- **Also contained in this folder is *MIDAS* (Marketing Information Data Analysis System), which contains confidential information on customers and processes and how Buckman associates interact with these customers to solve problems and improve their operations.**
- ***Customer Forums* allow a specific customer's employees worldwide the ability to communicate among themselves and with Buckman associates. Access to these forums is restricted to people who are specially nominated by Buckman and the customer. A separate "shadow" forum exists for each; accessible only to Buckman associates, the latter is invisible to the customer.**
- **The *Customer Information Center* (CIC) is an unstructured database used by front-line sales associates to store electronic copies of documents specific to a certain customer. Access to this data is restricted to the account representative and his/her manager, and other marketing support groups.**
- **The most recent addition to K'Netix is the BuLab Learning Center, which facilitates Buckman's distance learning project. This is in essence a distributive learning tool with interconnected networks of Notes databases. The purpose is to deliver asynchronous, just-in-time education and training to associates throughout the world.**

Every IT architecture has its drawbacks. Buckman's choice of systems and applications is dictated by need, not protocol. The IT architecture has evolved over time, using what's available off the shelf whenever possible to reduce capital expenses. "If we can buy it, we don't develop it," says Buckman. Each application has been chosen to fulfill a specific KM need, based on its inherent features.

An Internet approach, for example, would not work well for training, since the latter requires large amounts of data and graphics—thus long connect and download times. So for global access to just-in-time training, Buckman relies on LearningSpace from Lotus Development Inc., a distributive learning tool with interconnected networks of Notes databases.

Never judge a book by its cover, or a KM suite by its platform.

In contrast, Buckman's BuLab TechForum, one of seven forums—and "the engine of our knowledge sharing," as Buckman refers to it—is an off-the-shelf application provided by CompuServe. The application allows up to twenty-one different message and library sections, mostly topic-related.

Discussions proceed globally and directly, while at week's end, a "section leader" is charged with capturing conversation "threads" and posting them in a "library." By piggybacking CompuServe's application and global network reach, Buckman has worldwide connectivity at a fraction of the cost. All 1,200 associates have CompuServe IDs and passwords and they use the network for both intra- and intercompany communication. "It works anywhere anytime. From the desktop and from the laptops," says Koskiniemi.

Although the buy-not-build philosophy keeps infrastructure costs in check, K'Netix is certainly not cheap. Buckman spends about 3.75 percent of revenue on its integrated KM and IT activities each year, not including senior management time. The per-employee price tag is about $7,500, covering IT, telephone charges, hardware, and software licensee fees. But the benefits, in terms of improved customer contact and relationships, vastly outweigh the cost. "In total," says Koskiniemi, "we spend about $10 million. Can you spend more? Sure. Can you spend less? Sure. The key is that there is business we got that we would not have won if this system was not in place."

THE OTHER 95 PERCENT

Technology, however, is only 5 percent of the KM equation at Buckman. The idea of sharing knowledge, sometimes with across-the-ocean strangers one has never met, is "90 percent culture, 5 percent technology, and the rest is magic," says Buckman. Fortunately, Buckman labs had a sharing-oriented culture even before KM became a corporate strategy. The evidence is in its code of ethics:

1. The organization is composed of unique individuals with different capabilities, all necessary to successful operation of the company.
2. Individuality will be acknowledged by treating one another with dignity and respect and maintaining the focus on continuous and positive communication among all employees.
3. The contributions and accomplishments of all employees will be recognized irrespective of magnitude.

> Whereas respect and recognition are critical, they are not necessarily formalized in the manner of fatter paychecks or bigger bonuses at Buckman. Sharing is simply part of everyone's work. Forum Section Leaders, who either volunteer or are recruited for this weekly editing job, receive no special form of compensation. "The only status involved is the 'SL' at the end of your title," says Koskiniemi.

Top management sets the tone for sharing. "Some modes of encouragement have been more subtle than others," says Burrows. CEO Bob Buckman is known to have printed out weekly lists of TechForum participants. Associates who were not on the list would quickly get the message: "If I am not in there, sharing my knowledge, exactly what use am I to the organization?" says Burrows. At the same time, 1993's most active forum participants got a surprise trip to a conference in Arizona plus a $150 leather bag and an upgrade to an IBM Thinkpad 720. "Both have since become status symbols unto themselves," reveals Koskiniemi.

Bingo! To get folks to share, show them the way by sharing first.

The net result is that sharing has become endemic to the organization. Of course, some associates are more dedicated than others. It certainly helps that management leads by sharing: Bob Buckman was "sitting in the back of the room [at a meeting in Arizona] writing a synopsis as the meeting was unfolding to post in BuLab News as soon as it was over."

MEASURING SUCCESS

Buckman began its systematic KM and best practice transfer efforts with a clear goal in mind: It wanted to be able to get closer to its customers, faster. Consequently, the measurement of its KM initiatives centers on the interface with customers.

On an organizational (collective) knowledge level, Buckman measures the system's value in the number of customer contracts it helps the company win. It also measures its effectiveness through the growth in new product related revenues. In the four years prior to the launch of K'Netix in 1992, the average sales of products less than five years old was 23.6 percent of total sales. In the four years following K'Netix introduction the average rose to 33.3 percent. Buckman also credits much of its 250 percent growth in sales in the past decade to its on-line KM systems.

> "Since it involves the entire company to get an improvement of this magnitude and particularly on the interface with the customer, I believe that this is solid evidence of an ability to satisfy customers better and faster. In other words the productivity of the entire company went up," says CEO Bob Buckman.

On an individual-knowledge level, Buckman monitors the education of the portion of the work force engaged on the front line. Seventy-nine percent of them now have college degrees, up from 39 percent in 1979. At the time, Buckman's sales force numbered 79, compared to over 600 today.

Operational measures provide additional evidence of success:

- The speed of response to customers has increased; it now takes hours, not days.

- The quality of response has risen all over the world.
- On-line remote access to knowledge means the office is anywhere.
- Growth of talented people has increased; more employees are immersed in high-intensity projects.

Still skeptical? So were we, at first. But not after we looked at this list of big benefits!

"What used to take weeks, now takes hours. What used to take months, now takes a week," says Koskiniemi. "That means we are responding to the customer, faster." Ultimately, Buckman believes it impossible to put a dollar-and-cents figure on its knowledge network. Rather, it is more a central tenet to the way the company as a whole operates. "Do you want to measure it before you get into it?" asks Koskiniemi. "Not really. I think you just do it, and measure later. If you wait for the measure to take action, you may find it is too late."

Chapter 15

TI'S BEST PRACTICE SHARING ENGINE

Slimmed down, reorganized, and restructured, Texas Instruments entered the early 1990s looking for a new way to generate performance improvement. Building on their initial success in sharing best practices across semiconductor fabrication plants, TI's CEO, president, and chairman of the board, Jerry Junkins (now deceased), launched a companywide improvement and transfer program in 1994.

The story of KM thinking at Texas Instruments is the of story of post-reengineering management thinking in corporate America. Like many of its peers, the Dallas-based electronics company (1996 sales: $13.1 billion) reengineered, reorganized, and restructured during the late 1980s and early 1990s. With over 50,000 employees in sixteen countries worldwide, it has empowered its workers and delayered its corporate body.

What do you do when you're done cutting? You start managing.

"We had cut and cut and cut," says Cindy Johnson, director of Collaboration and Knowledge Sharing and a fifteen-year veteran of the company. "We had achieved high levels of efficiency across our operations by streamlining our processes and fine tuning our people and resources." Then, in 1993, with the last drop of fat squeezed out of its organizational cost structure, TI began to look elsewhere for performance improvement. The company's focus shifted from cost cutting to opportunity growth.

With that shift, "we felt we needed to find a new paradigm for reaching the next level of improvement," says Johnson. "We had to find ways to become more agile and learn faster so that we can innovate faster than our competitors," she explains. "This is not about cutting people or bringing in new machines. It is about facilitating the flow of ideas, practices, and knowledge."

KNOWING WHAT WE KNOW

In 1993 Junkins challenged the Quality Leadership Team (QLT, a team of senior executives from each TI business) to create a common and global approach to business excellence. "We had pockets of mediocrity right next door to world-class performance simply because one operation did not know what was happening at the other operation," explains Johnson. The QLT's goal was to find a way to level the internal playing field and leverage best performance across the enterprise.

Out of this need, TI-BEST, or the TI Business Excellence Strategy, was born. TI-BEST deploys a standardized process of defining business excellence, assessing progress, identifying improvement opportunities, and establishing and deploying an action. "TI-BEST provides a common methodology and a common language that can be used to provide best practices across the company and to more rapidly accelerate best practice," explained Junkins at a 1994 leadership conference. "We cannot tolerate having world-class performance right next to mediocre performance simply because we don't have a method to implement best practices."

Junkins laid the groundwork just before his tragic death in 1996 on a business trip to Europe. But the effort continued full steam under the guidance of incoming CEO Tom Engibous, former head of the company's semiconductor group. Engibous embraced TI-BEST, and in 1994 he challenged his managers of TI's thirteen wafer fabrication plants to come up with a way to close down the wide gaps in their plants' yields and productivity levels.

After one year of sharing best practices, TI generated $500 million in "free" fab capacity. Need we say any more?

At the time, the semiconductor market was tight and new capacity came at a premium. A new wafer fab would cost between $500 million and $1 billion to construct. If TI could eke out the capacity equal to that of a wafer fab by bringing laggard plants up to snuff, it would save significantly as well as be able to provide much-needed product to its customers at a time of need.

The managers, along with a team of facilitators (trained in process redesign theory and cycle time reduction techniques) compared best practices across wafer fab plants globally. Combined with best practices gained from external benchmarking, they then created a "virtual fab" (read: a best practice). They created an incentive to work together by tying their bonuses to total capacity and productivity measures. These improvements generated one "free" fab of capacity that same year—and then, they did it again in 1994 and 1995.

TRY, TRY AGAIN

Impressed with the success of the wafer-fab effort, top management throughout TI began realizing the potential cultural and financial benefits of internal best practice sharing. The insight sparked a flurry of enterprisewide activities.

By October of 1994, TI launched the Best Practice Sharing Initiative to help shift the internal culture from "I have to solve my own problems" to one of looking for existing solutions—first. "Only invent the wheel once!" was the rallying cry.

In October 1994, the QLT chartered a Best Practice Sharing Team and the TI Office of Best Practices (OBP) to help facilitate, guide, and manage the sharing of internal knowledge among the company's vast and widespread operations. The team's mandate was to design the sharing process and IT infrastructure. The OBP serves as the "engine" for developing and deploying training and technology; it is supported by a team of thirteen champions and a network of 138 global facilitators.

"Facilitators devote about 10 to 50 percent of their time to sharing," Johnson explains. "Their role is to identify existing strengths within TI, document those practices that provide improvement, and share them throughout the organization. They are matchmakers," says Johnson. "They are trying to broker their businesses' strengths to help others and in return, learn about practices in other businesses."

SHIFTING GEARS

The role of a facilitator or "knowledge broker" was created in TI based on the "free" wafer fab Findings as well as Gabriel Szulanski's research conducted at the French business school, INSEAD, and sponsored by APQC. A third party helps smooth the transfer of knowledge from giver to recipient.

Indeed, TI's greatest challenge has been motivating people to share and accept other people's ideas. In an organization where engineers take pride in innovation, relying on someone else's work has not always been respected practice. It was up to OBP to change that perception. "What we see over and over again is that you have to provide the focus and motivation, and you have to provide the tools, and then you have to reward and create an incentive structure," says Johnson of the cultural transformation.

Invested in reengineering? Do not despair! Lessons learnt once need not be learnt again. The result: a faster step up the ladder.

In some respects, TI was fortunate. Years of reengineering and cross-functional teamwork provided a strong basis on which to build the practice of sharing. "We understand processes, we talk to each other, and we use the same language," says Johnson. These are all critical components of a knowledge-enabling culture. However, reengineering had left its scars as well. TI—like many other organizations—has lost an entire layer of middle management, and with it a critical link in the communication chain. Fortunately, new network technologies have stepped in to recreate the links.

"Technology has given us new ways to keep in touch with each other and share information. We have to take advantage of that technology to get better faster," says Johnson. Before intranets and Lotus Notes, knowledge bases were slow, tedious, and typically not easily searched. "We could create enormous repositories, but never get anything out of them," she muses. Search engines, digital signals, and data compression have made high-speed communication cheap and easy. The first release of the TI's internal card catalogue, in April 1995, took only a quarter to design and roll out. "Previously, such effort would have taken at least two years."

THE BEST PRACTICE "CARD CATALOG"

The technology heart of TI's knowledge management efforts is a Best Practices KnowledgeBase—a Lotus Notes application accessed through

CREATING A KNOWLEDGE-ENABLING IT ARCHITECTURE

Based on her experience in helping develop and implement the knowledge-enabling technology at TI, Johnson offers the following five tips:

1. **Find a renaissance person who thinks in business processes and is also technology savvy. Work through a basic KM model: First capture, then abstract, then disseminate.**
2. **Assess what tools provide the best capabilities in each area of the process, using cost, maturity, and features as your assessment criteria. Recognize that you will need to stabilize new technologies and deploy them worldwide.**
3. **Challenge your team "not to design the IT solution" but to focus on the process, roles, and culture change requirements. After each work session, go back and develop a prototype that illustrates the process defined in the session. Force team members to focus on the future state and not the technology.**
4. **Build an implementation plan around your proposed solution—don't take on training for the technology as a whole. TI's initial implementation was a Notes-based solution, and training only focused on the best practices sharing application and provided just enough training to get everyone up and running.**
5. **Stand back and watch the darts fly over your choice of technology. Be prepared to answer any and all questions about that choice. Don't oversell your technology or let it become a religious battle. Stay ahead of your critics.**

TI's global intranet. The choice of Notes reflects TI's belief that the groupware provides the best categorization capability. In March 1995, two hundred TI Notes users began using the KnowledgeBase. The facilitators, the Best Practice Team, and the QLT loaded the original supply of best practices; to date, the database contains more than five hundred practices.

Each practice is documented using a title, a short narrative, and contact information. Facilitators assign a quality criterion from a list of eight derived from the Malcolm Baldrige National Quality Awards, the European Foundation for Quality Management, and the Singapore Quality Award Criteria. Practices are then categorized by process, from a list of sixteen high-level processes (based on a classification framework developed by the APQC and Arthur Andersen). Each practice is also assigned keywords from a list of 130 predefined keywords that apply to the process. (Users can perform keyword or a full-text search to locate relevant practices.)

TI packs a "mean" one-two punch: One for Lotus Notes. Two for the intranet.

The Best Practice KnowledgeBase also contains external best practices and benchmarking information. A Notes-based project notebook helps teams capture learning and knowledge created during the course of a project, and a Notes-based discussion database enables employees to communicate business gaps and solutions.

While the Notes KnowledgeBase allows limited access, an intranet site called "ShareIt" was launched in July of 1995 using the InterNotes Publisher. The site allows TI's employees worldwide access to the best practices listed in its database, as well as many of the Notes databases. Using Domino to bridge the Notes/Web gap, users can access the Notes material via any WWW browser. "Shareit" now gets more than 10,000 hits per month.

TI has launched another Internet application, a "yellow pages" web site, Connect, which lists TI employees' contact information, experience, knowledge, and interests. It also contains want ads, which will allow employees to promote new business opportunities and improvement projects for their peers to review, as well as to solicit ideas and resources for solving problems.

WE'VE COME A LONG WAY

After three full years of operation, the Office of Best Practices has multiple successes under its collective belt: It has provided an integrated mechanism for best practices sharing, built the initial supply of catalogued practices to more than 500, and increased awareness and demand for the KnowledgeBase across the company.

In the process, it has learned four key lessons:

- Do what you are able to do.
- Don't try to do it all at one time.

- Have the infrastructure already in place and connecting the knowledge management activities to your business strategy.
- Put more emphasis on like-skilled communities (i.e., software groups and purchasing expertise). Implementation is more likely to take place where there is commonality.

The three pillars of KM excellence:
1. Focus 2. Focus 3. Focus

TI would like to pursue knowledge management on a wider scale. In the early stages of its KM initiative, TI focused on achieving operational excellence by sharing best practices across businesses. However, Johnson recognizes a shift is already underway toward collaboration for

SPREADING THE WORD: "SHAREFAIR"

TI's Best Practice Sharing Program recognizes that providing knowledge-enabling technology does not guarantee people will share or use preexisting knowledge. In many high-tech companies—and TI is no exception—the inherent culture is one of designing new solutions, not reusing old ones. Indeed, the latter may be considered antithetical.

In June 1996, TI held its first companywide ShareFair. The one-day event drew over 500 people, who attended seminars on how to share knowledge and visited an exhibit hall of more than fifty best practices (the "practice that's best for me"). Among them were best practices in business process management, customer satisfaction survey techniques, strategic planning process, and user-centered product development process.

At the ShareFair, TI also handed out its first "Not Invented Here, But I Did It Anyway" (NIHBIDIA) Award to the sources and recipient of a transfer that exemplified the cultural change at TI through the transfer of a practice. Nominations for the award were evaluated for business impact, business improvement priority, span of the transfer, and method of transfer. The judges' panel put greatest emphasis on high impact, high priority, broad implementation, and team approach.

Fifty-two nominations were submitted with over 450 team members cited for generating savings in excess of $1 billion. In the end, awards were given to two TI organizations which best illustrated the spirit of best practice sharing through their transfer of clean-room best practices

innovation in product development and increased customer intimacy as the focal points of its KM efforts. "The key message is the focus message," says Johnson. "You can't take KM and say we are to become a 'knowledge-creating company.' You have to find the key leverage points before you do anything else."

between a semiconductor wafer fab and the defense business gallium arsenide wafer fab.

The 1997 ShareFair focused on Internet Technologies and the sharing of best practices in the use of the intranet, extranet, and Internet capabilities. The 1997 NIHBIDIA Award generated fifty-one nominations with over 480 team members cited. The award was given to TI's Dallas Wafer Fab Operations, and to a new TI acquisition, Silicon Systems Incorporated, for their sharing of wafer fab practices.

The TI ShareFairs have helped employees recognize the value of reusing existing knowledge and have attached prestige and status to the practice. Future cultural transformation efforts will focus on helping employees:

- **Rely on the Best Practices KnowledgeBase first for a solution to their business gaps**
- **Become aware of others' problems to see if assistance can be offered**
- **Collaborate to solve a common business gap for which there is not an existing solution document, instead of attempting to solve it separately**
- **Operate at the same level of excellence across the organization**

To achieved these goals, TI recognizes it must change the way it rewards and compensates its employees to reflect the great emphasis on sharing and reuse. Indeed, the best practice sharing team hopes to make Best Practice Sharing an integral part of individual, organizational, and business review.

Chapter 16

BECOMING A "KNOWLEDGE BANK"

In its global battle against poverty and economic malaise, the World Bank can afford to waste no time. The Bank has designed a comprehensive KM initiative to improve the process of best practice sharing among its regional groups. By formalizing hitherto informal communities of practice, linking regional groups, and leveraging the unifying powers of technology, the Bank wants to become a superior knowledge performer in-house first. Ultimately, it hopes to be a clearinghouse for economic development knowledge—"what works and what doesn't and the data to prove it"—throughout the world.

In the fall of 1996, James Wolfensohn, president of the World Bank, pronounced knowledge management a strategic thrust for the twenty-first century. Speaking before 175 finance ministers, Wolfensohn outlined his vision for the World Bank of the future. "The Bank Group's relationships with governments and institutions all over the world and our unique reservoir of development experience across sectors and countries position us to play a leading role in [a] new knowledge partnership," said Wolfensohn. "To capture this potential we need to invest in the necessary systems that will enhance our ability to gather development information and experience and share it with our clients. We need to become, in effect, the 'Knowledge Bank.'"

Make note of this: Using a clear blueprint first prevents chaos later!

Within months of Wolfensohn's speech, an institutional task force translated his grand vision into a comprehensive action plan and detailed a road map for organizational restructuring. (Of course, they benchmarked best practices with APQC first!) The Bank's new KM system is in early stages of implementation, but management anticipates that it will dramatically change the way in which it operates internally and interacts externally. Based on early returns from a few grass-roots guerrilla pilots, they are probably right.

Initially, the supranational is focusing on internal knowledge; it wants to provide all of its employees with "just-in-time, just-enough" knowledge to perform their work better.

What does that mean? It means advisory services would get answers to customers, faster, by accessing existing knowledge and best practices from around the globe. The institutionwide effort will also make it easier for the Bank to consolidate its comparative advantage in providing international best practice. Plus, the more efficient use of existing resources will increase its capacity for serving multiple stakeholders, be they borrowers, donors, or foundations.

Ultimately, the bank hopes to become a *clearinghouse* of knowledge on economic development by opening up its collective IQ to external browsers and interconnecting with universities, foundations, and others.

This list of mission and business objectives would not surprise anyone familiar with the Bank. Though its mission tends toward the altruistic, the Bank is managed for commercial viability. Headed by a practical ex-Wall Street executive, this financial powerhouse generates approximately $1 billion in annual profits and maintains a pristine credit rating, while lending between $15 and $20 billion a year to some eighty developing nations. The decision to embrace KM, therefore, is rooted in sound business principles—turning internal know-how into commercial success, achieving operational excellence, and forming more intimate ties with external customers.

"After fifty years of providing lending and advisory services in every region of the world, the Bank Group is a substantial repository of development experience and best practice," explains Stephen Denning, program director, Knowledge Management. However, he points out, "this knowledge is not always easily available to those who need it when they need it, or in formats they find useful and accessible. As a result, the effectiveness of our service suffers."

THINK BIG, START SMALL

Like other organizations, the Bank was not altogether a KM novice when it embarked on this recent campaign. Over the years, the organization has taken steps toward more effective management of knowledge, including the highly successful African Region LDB, a smart, live database of economic indicators and country-specific information. All of the pre-1996 efforts, however, were characterized by their local focus and attention to the elemental aspects of knowledge (i.e., data and information vs. action-oriented, best practice knowledge). Further, they did not provide the basis for a sustainable, integrated strategy. "The fragmentation associated with continuing or further proliferation of local knowledge systems would delay by years the Bank's efforts to create the Knowledge Partnership," says Denning.

This is one case where the "more" is not the "better."

The organizationwide initiative began in earnest after Bank executives participated in an APQC's KM 1995–96 consortium benchmarking study (APQC, 1996). Armed with Wolfensohn's vision and newly gathered best practices in KM, the Bank appointed Denning to the newly created position of program director, Knowledge Management, and devised a grand plan, involving new organizational facets, such as sector networks and help desks (see page 166) and a phased implementation plan that takes incremental steps toward the *knowledge bank* ideal.

LAUNCHING PILOTS

By September of 1996, the Bank was ready to roll out its first sector network: EKMS, the Education Knowledge Management System. With a core staff of twenty and located within the Human Development Group, EKMS serves 250–300 education sector staff worldwide. Its purpose is to facilitate knowledge synthesis, stimulate discussion, and identify areas that need attention. For example, its staff organized a popular e-mail discussion on the use of local languages in textbooks. It then distilled key learnings which were added to the organization's knowledge bank.

The EKMS staff identifies existing best practices, especially through its advisory groups, and provides training for education staff. Groups of two to four people work on each of nine strategic focus areas, such as economics of education, educational technology, and effective schools and teachers. In addition, groups of six to twelve of the Bank's education professionals located throughout the world act as advisers on each of the focus areas as part of their full-time duties.

The EKMS network is prototypical to the Bank's emerging sector networks. At its nexus is the intersection of technology and people. An internal Web site provides staff with access to documented knowledge such as best practice examples, tools, ideas, links to other Internet sites, key readings, and selected documents. An Advisory Service—a help desk staffed by two information specialists—complements the abundance of formal, organized knowledge by providing answers to specific questions. Information specialists take responsibility for making sure internal "clients" get the information they need, whenever possible—even performing specialized research.

Let us repeat this one: *"Network building is relationship building."*

"Many people initially said, 'I don't know how the Sector Network can help me,'" Martha Pattillo-Siv, coordinator for the Education Advisory Service, explains. "But once they saw they had someplace to turn to get their specific questions answered, the network took on a different texture for them." Says Pattillo-Siv: "Network building is relationship building, and you really cannot build a relationship through a Web site alone."

As an added benefit, Advisory Service staff deliver detailed records of questions and answers to enrich the organization's collective IQ. Previously, no such record existed, and each question ignited a "reinvention of the wheel" process that significantly slowed down response time to external customers. "By tracking this information, we ensure that the momentum does not stop after every question," Pattillo-Siv says. "We see where the trends and gaps are. Then we can build knowledge development projects based on those gaps."

About 15 percent of the World Bank's education staff routinely uses the Advisory Service each week. Though a relatively small percentage, it sits well with the Bank's "think big, but start small" approach. "We do not want to be like the restaurant that gets great reviews from the *New York Times* and is mobbed with enthusiastic customers before it is really ready to handle them," Pattillo-Siv jokes.

Furthermore, the impact even on this smaller scale is already noticeable. Pattillo-Siv recalls a recent case of a staff member in Nepal who called the Advisory Service looking for implementation plan models to help his clients in the Nepalese Ministry of Education prepare the next phase of a primary education project. "Through its networks, the Advisory Service was able to find a generic implementation plan as well as multiple contacts in countries that had done similar projects," recalls Pattillo-Siv. The Advisory Service located people in Hungary and Turkey with best practice experiences in rolling out similar education projects. "The EKMS was able to rapidly pull together resources from around World Bank, where in the past there would have been no way to facilitate this kind of sharing."

FIGURING OUT THE RESISTANCE POINTS

The Bank's KM initiative is in the early stages of implementation. Its KM staff, however, has been able to identify seven organizational resistance points that could potentially impede their progress:

- **Shifting the culture towards sharing**
- **Setting and implementing quality standards**
- **Maintaining the system to avoid knowledge "junkyards"**
- **Ensuring that the system stays demand-driven**
- **Balancing new information versus better access to current information**
- **Resolving external issues, such as confidentiality**
- **Achieving an integrated approach across the organization**

BUILDING THE LAUNCH PAD

While the sector networks gear up, the Bank's IT function is busy constructing a supportive technology infrastructure. "Knowledge management is 80 percent human brain power and 20 percent facilitation by information technology," says Denning. "The challenge is to harness the technology to link people together and to leverage its impact for development." In practical terms, the Bank's challenge is twofold: pulling together disparate knowledge bases so that knowledge can flow seamlessly throughout the organization and harnessing the right technology for leveraging particular aspects of knowledge.

The World Bank's KM technology infrastructure is not a single monolithic delivery system. Rather, it is a suite of tools, mostly running on Lotus Notes and Web-site platforms, which pulls together a collection of integrated knowledge resources. The Bank tries to match technology with knowledge "typologies" and is working to accommodate multiple access alternatives, from faxes to telephones. In some parts of the world, modem access is nearly impossible.

To accommodate both *divergent* and *convergent* knowledge processes, the Bank's IT architecture will include (in descending order of "knowledge" intensity):

For best results: take one spoon of low-tech, and one spoon of high-tech, mix and drink.

- *Databases*, having vast warehousing capacity and relational logic, will offer access to codified knowledge, including terms of reference, consultants, who knows what, lessons learned, key articles and books, and reports.
- *Knowledge bases*, accessible via Web sites or Lotus Notes, will contain best practice reservoirs, including sector strategies, tool kits, model outputs, analytical tools, sources of subject-driven information, and think-pieces.
- *Help desks*, low-tech and manned by experienced "humans," will provide the intelligent capacity to answer complex queries, and to customize resource maps and information packets based on specialized needs.

AN ARCHIPELAGO OF TECHNOLOGY ISLANDS

When it came time to create the technology skeleton that would support the growing body of knowledge, the Bank ran into a common corporate problem: Years of as-needed technological and content development have resulted in an IT landscape resembling a veritable archipelago of disconnected islands. Each sector (department) has had its own somewhat different way of viewing, processing, and storing knowledge.

For the Bank's Information Technology Services (ITS) the challenge has been to develop an architecture that would accommodate diverse knowledge models but have enough commonality to allow best practices to be easily transferred. Initially, it appeared the knowledge

A BLUEPRINT FOR THE FUTURE

Transformation without guidance often results in chaos. And the World Bank was indeed careful to draw a detailed blueprint of the "knowledge bank" of the future before it began tearing up departmental walls and designing enterprisewide systems. This sketch depicted a three-tier, knowledge-enabling infrastructure.

Tier 1: The Sector Networks. The key operating units of the KM plan, the Sector Networks are formalized versions of the bank's informal, international communities of practice. Whereas many sectors—such as infrastructure or environment—have had informal communities of practice for years, they had been mostly focused on country or regional expertise. The Sector Networks, in contrast, will expand and formalize these relationships beyond geographic boundaries.

Sector Networks will take the lead in developing the requisite knowledge bases, i.e., organizing operational staff so that the flow of global knowledge is facilitated. Each knowledge area will be led by a full-time knowledge manager and supported by subject specialists and other operational staff, who will spend part of their time building and maintaining the knowledge base—constituting communities of practice in their fields of expertise—assisted by help desk personnel.

Tier 2: Central Knowledge Management Team. While the networks must continue to do the bank's day-to-day work, a Central Knowledge Management Team with dedicated full-time staff will be charged with overseeing the ongoing health of the knowledge management efforts. The team's responsibilities include:

- **Establishing and integrating knowledge management framework**
- **Setting priorities among multiple knowledge management activities**
- **Managing external access to the KM system**
- **Regulating the knowledge economy**
- **Managing issues related to the quality of knowledge**
- **Consolidating external knowledge partnerships**

domains were simply too differentiated and any compromise would, in all likelihood, stifle creativity within each domain. At the same time, merely overlaying this archipelago with a common Web-based browser interface would provide some measure of pseudo-integration but would deprive users of more systematic and powerful access of a truly integrated system.

• Facilitating the organizational cultural shift

Tier 3: IT Services. Finally, the Bank's ITS group will support the knowledge management system with the appropriate technological infrastructure, ensuring the knowledge management system is fully integrated with other information systems in the organization.
Remaining Regional Role. While the networks and the central teams are either new or newly formalized facets designed to cut across the global organization, the existing regional structure will continue to play an important role, including:

- ***Network management:*** **As members of the Network Councils and Sector Boards, managers from the regions will play a crucial role in championing the knowledge management initiative and in fostering the culture shift.**
- ***Network staff:*** **The regional staff, who constitute the bulk of the network, will be the main actors in the knowledge management activities.**
- ***Budget:*** **Roughly one-third of the incremental budget resources for networks will be devoted to knowledge management activities.**
- ***Live data bases:*** **The regions will play a key role in developing and maintaining the live databases.**
- ***Region- and country-specific knowledge:*** **The regions will play a unique role in capturing and managing region- and country-specific knowledge. Details have still to be worked out.**
- ***Mission briefing and debriefing:*** **The regions should play a key role in knowledge capture through mission briefing and debriefing. Details have still to be worked out.**
- ***Help desks:*** **The regions will play a role (still to be defined) in organizing help desk functions.**
- ***External knowledge partnerships:*** **Most of the regions are undertaking or planning knowledge partnerships with organizations in their respective regions.**

A closer look revealed that while domains stored, processed, and viewed data differently, they all used more or less the same basic building blocks to classify their explicit knowledge. The solution was to add in a third layer of user interface into the bank's IT architecture. This interface is designed to fetch data from divergent databases, and present it within a context that is familiar to the particular user.

WEIGHING RISKS AND REWARDS

No one said it would be easy. . . . But no KM is going to make it 10× harder.

The Bank's staff recognizes KM is in its infancy and presents tall challenges—in particular in terms of creating a new culture of sharing (see page 164). However, these challenges are dwarfed by the risks inherent in failing to manage knowledge, and the benefits of managing it more effectively, which include:

- Higher levels of knowledge reuse
- Reduction or elimination of rework
- Increased quality and quantity of client services through enhanced access to Bank knowledge
- Strengthened comparative advantage in providing international best practice
- Stronger capacity building
- A prerequisite for physical decentralization
- Better incentives for excellence

While some benefits may not show up for some time, a 1996 survey of Bank employees revealed even early KM efforts to be yielding positive results. Close to 90 percent of employees have found KM-related products and services useful or very useful; some 84 percent rated the turnaround as fast or very fast; and 70 percent find that it makes their work significantly more effective.

The Bank's initial focus has been on retooling its internal operations to improve sharing of best practices. The pilot EKMS network has already been joined by three other sector network pilot systems—for nutrition, health, and population. By the end of fiscal year 1998, the Bank planned to have seven or eight sector families taking their first systematic steps toward KM. The rest will join by the end of the following fiscal year.

Longer-term, the Bank's vision is fixed on building knowledge partnerships with external stakeholders. "If we can do that for our in-house staff, why not make it directly available to our clients and partners as well?" asks Denning. "If we are working with joint information, we are solving a joint problem. The whole concept of having genuine partnership then becomes a real possibility."

Chapter 17

SEQUENT COMPUTER'S KNOWLEDGE "SLINGSHOT"

Aware that loyal customers value its knowledgeable sales force as much as its top-of-the-line UNIX systems, Sequent Computers began managing knowledge like an asset in 1993. The company's first step was building an enterprisewide technology infrastructure. Next it created a supportive organizational structure. Owning an earnings growth rate of 20 percent per year, Sequent clearly has no time to spare on reinventing the wheel.

For centuries, the smaller have relied on wits and agility to defeat larger opponents. Add a modern-day "slingshot" in the form of top-notch technology architecture, and you've got Sequent Computer Systems: This $600 million David competes with Goliath-size HP, IBM, DEC, and Sun Microsystems in the high end of the UNIX systems market. "With the kind of competition we have," says Roger Swanson, manager, Corporate Research Services at Sequent, "We have to act and look bigger than we are, and the only way to do that is by sharing information."

• Think Big • Act Fast • Be Smart

Based in Beaverton Oregon, Sequent employs 2,700 in fifty-three field locations in the United States, Europe, and Asia. It's gained a stellar reputation for being the "freightliner" of the UNIX world—perfect for those who require real "heavy-duty" machinery. But Sequent is not selling "big iron." It provides solutions, and often multimillion-dollar solutions. As such, the expertise of employees has become as critical to its success as the processing prowess of its computers.

"We recognized—or rather, our customers told us—that we were valued for the ability to de-risk complex multi-vendor IT projects because of our [knowledge-intensive] design and implementation expertise," says Marc Demarest, ex-chief knowledge officer. "We [the COO and CKO] became convinced very quickly that (1) we need to husband and nurture it [our knowledge] better, (2) we needed to amplify its effectiveness by making the tacit explicit and embodied, and by disseminating the embodiments, and (3) we needed to treat it as the asset it was from a corporate management perspective."

LET THERE BE KNOWLEDGE

Sequent began by carefully analyzing its business model. The goal was to identify and target *knowledge-sensitive points* where improvement would yield the greatest results. Was it reduced cycle time? Lower costs? Higher volume of customers, projects, and therefore revenue? Risk mitigation? Or what?

The analysis revealed Sequent would do best by focusing on its direct sales channel which includes professional services communities and sales teams. "Since these were close to revenue, the customer, and our cultural heart, they made a good starting point," says Demarest.

Customer intimacy means pushing intelligence to the front lines.

An added bonus: They are also the closest to Sequent's competitors—and hence a logical place to make a differentiating impact. "The best and smartest people must be on the front lines dealing with the customer," explains Swanson. Indeed, Sequent had realized that the productivity of its sales force was directly related to the number of years they've worked at the company. Experienced sales teams drew on their own knowledge reservoir to make future sales better and faster. The goal, therefore, was to make this knowledge available to everyone so that each front-line employee would be able to respond to customers with the collective intelligence of the organization.

PROVIDING THE UNDERPINNINGS

So, where to start? Based on a straightforward knowledge model which tracks knowledge through *construction*, *embodiment*, *dissemination*, and *use*, Sequent decided to focus on managing the two middle phases first.

"Embodiment and dissemination are the two most tractable," explains Swanson. They are also the ones most clearly in the organizational versus individual domain.

To implement its design, Sequent has followed a four-phased management strategy:

1. *Underpin* the efforts by providing the IT infrastructure—a common space for storing and retrieving document-based knowledge and some forms of electronic discussions
2. *Observe* the knowledge economy to understand what people use, what they contribute, and the feedback they provide to help fine-tune the system
3. *Measure* activities within the knowledge economy, such as patterns of use
4. *Orchestrate* by engineering more sophisticated social expectations about use, adding new content, new producer communities, and new tools

"We did one thing first: We built out the technology infrastructure we would use for all our KM initiatives," says Demarest, "because KM infrastructure is a must if you intend to instrument your knowledge economies. If you don't build it first, it will be built in pieces by dozens of people and projects and you will have a massive second-order integration problem trying to hook disparate systems together, so massive that its costs and inefficiencies might undo whatever improvements you get from KM programs."

At the core of Sequent's knowledge-enabling IT design is SCEL. Pronounced "sell," this is the Sequent Corporate Electronic Library, focusing on marketing and sales support and generally helping all employees do their jobs better. The SCEL vision is: "The one place to go to find anything you need to help you do your job more effectively." SCEL is an intranet site that contains corporate and individual knowledge domains (see page 173). The site is integrated with other Sequent applications, such as an on-line pricebook, the corporate "white pages," and a customer database. "It's a single holistic platform," says Swanson. E-mail discussions on shared

Seeking balance? Sequent chose centralized IT to offset a free-market KM philosophy.

"aliases" (discussion forums) are treated as "documents" and archived in SCEL.

Whereas SCEL is critical to the dissemination of knowledge, IT and KM are separate functions, one reporting to the CIO and the other to the manager of corporate research services. The IT organization provides the technology, and human and financial resources to support KM programs (current costs per employee, per year, are under $1,000). The manager of corporate research services has global responsibility for all knowledge management programs and infrastructure. A cross-functional SCEL design team consists of librarians, a Web master, programmers, a SCEL architect, a SCEL evangelist, and other members who provide linkage to other parts of the organization. This SCEL design team provides infrastructure, education, operational support, and KM program management and coordination, and acts as the keepers and guidance support system for the knowledge management effort. The KM function is also responsible for the company's patent portfolio and for such traditional corporate research services as the corporate library.

WHAT'S ON SCEL?

We think of SCEL as a city: a marketplace in which many vendors set up stores of various sorts and vend their knowledge to the consumer community.
—Marc Demarest, former CKO

The Sequent Computer Electronic Library is an internal, Web-based system for capturing, archiving, and providing information to Sequent employees. SCEL includes a combination of database management systems, full-text retrieval engines, file system storage, and complex clusters of programs, all of which are integrated into Sequent's worldwide internal Web and accessible to all employees through Web browsers.

The choice of an intranet application was a natural one, says Demarest. "Unlike Lotus Notes or other proprietary software, the Web is owned by no one," he says. As a result, Sequent is not beholden to any vendor for the migration path of its knowledge-enabling tools. The Web can be used for everything from real-time collaboration to electronic commerce. "It's the infrastructure of choice of computing inside and outside the firm for the next decade," he says.

SCEL works on a publisher/consumer relationship. Every employee is a publisher and/or consumer if they use SCEL. Publishers put knowledge into the system and consumers use that knowledge. "We take, deliberately, a laissez-faire capitalist approach to the 'what content' question: user demand and producer marketing savvy determine content availability," says Demarest. "We do not, and do not intend to, regulate content centrally. We are responsible for providing a safe, clean, well-planned city, not for acting as a knowledge police force."

Indeed, the SCEL team relies on market mechanisms to control quality: consumers complain when the content is bad. Every primary section or page in SCEL contains a feedback button to allow consumers to immediately react to good or poor documents as well as system features. User feedback goes *directly* to the publisher. A copy also goes to the SCEL team, who monitors it for action. When the market mechanisms do not work, and the knowledge is considered high-value by the librarians, the design team or the KM team will intervene.

When Sequent began to build SCEL in 1995, it brought together groups of "influencers" from across the company to understand the way people thought information should be organized. The design team uncovered two views. Business and marketing groups clustered information around the value chain and groupings such as "customer," "products," "competitors," and "suppliers." Other groups preferred a more functional view of the organization. SCEL was subsequently designed to accommodate both views, by relying on HTML documents and hyperlinks. After they opt for a value-chain or functional overview, users can browse or search, using a standard, key-word–driven Web search engine.

The SCEL publishers began populating the content areas with "magnet" content such as outstanding presentations, strategy and scripts for sales calls, and design documents which people wanted but could not get elsewhere except by going directly to the author. This approach has positioned SCEL, from day one, as the place to find high value knowledge. And, although in early days the SCEL team would send e-mails suggesting users consult SCEL for particular knowledge needs, very quickly it has become corporate norm to expect to find important information in SCEL. Now, when users cannot find what they need, they are quick to complain, thus proving the productive forces of demand-side economies.

SCEL provides the dissemination infrastructure for both semistructured and structured content. Structured content includes alpha-numeric data which can be stored in conventional relational databases. Semi-structured content, such as pictures, presentations, spreadsheets, and mail messages is managed by storing the structuring containers and metadata about the containers.

Metadata is captured on a per-document basis by the publication infrastructure and is stored in a centralized database "behind" the SCEL server itself. Obviously, standard metadata like author, title, subject, keywords, document type, and so forth are captured. There is an effort in progress on the Web, led by library scientists, to come up with a uniform metadata classification scheme, and, when and if that effort produces something, Sequent will consider adopting it.

SCEL also provides ways for disseminating or embodying unstructured knowledge. In the case of full-motion video, that means metadata-based descriptions, until the software technology capable of "querying" such containers is robust.

It also means creating mechanisms such as *hypermail*, which help push unstructured content into the "searcheable realm." Hypermail is a simple archiving technology that captures conversation threads in electronic chat forums based on their "subject" matter line. When a conversation is started with an "alias" (the Sequent term for an e-mail distribution list), the subject matter of the first e-mail becomes the topic, and every subsequent message is threaded on to the main message, thus forming a small question-answer group of messages.

Each set of threaded messages is stored under its alias for reference. When messages are read later for the purpose of information gathering, the consumer may contribute to the group of messages by using the same subject topic so that his response is threaded in that set of messages. Messages are not edited for accuracy. If there is incorrect information in any of the messages, it is corrected by the group itself or by others in the company using the feedback button.

Release 3.0

Sequent has recently installed SCEL 3.0. The fifth iteration of the original SCEL 1.0 roll-out in the first quarter of 1995, the new release has much higher publishing capabilities. In addition, Sequent plans to bring down SCEL's external walls by creating other areas like SPEL (the Partner Library) which serve constituencies outside the corporation and allow them to have limited views of the company's internal knowledge bases. This system is more porous and allows more publishing import and export than before but still maintains security and firewalls.

A "LAISSEZ-FAIRE" KM PHILOSOPHY

In contrast with the planned and centralized manner with which Sequent developed its organizational and IT infrastructure, the company's approach to content and practice is decidedly hands-off. Both are allowed to evolve without any "government" (read *corporate*) interference.

"It always amazes me that we want capitalism everywhere but inside our own firms," notes Demarest. "The whole point of KM is that no one—most definitely not some wonk with the title CKO in corporate HQ—is in a position to understand the hundreds of different, specific contexts in which knowledge is required to satisfy a customer or business partner."

Hence the knowledge economy at Sequent is regulated by the twin market forces of supply and demand. An electronic hot link (the feedback button) on each page allows readers to inform publishers whether their knowledge meets quality standards, and how helpful it's been. Sequent uses a push-pull system (so does Texas Instruments). "'Push-based,' centrally planned economies (such as the former Soviet Union) don't work well," notes Demarest. Furthermore, "adult learning theories suggest that people learn best when their learning experiences are contextualized, that is, when they learn 'just in time.'" Sequent's "pull" system is designed to put control of the knowledge bases in the hands of consumers, and permits optimal learning to take place.

Not surprisingly, Sequent does not offer specific KM-related compensation. Prestige is the currency of greatest value. Prestige comes from being seen as an expert, and expertise is a "reward" for producing high-value knowledge that is useful to consumers. Not using SCEL to do your work would be as strange and antisocial a behavior as not retrieving your voice- or e-mail.

OBSERVE FIRST, MEASURE LATER

By its own admission—and reflective of its libertarian bent—Sequent has spent less time on measuring results than on understanding and enabling the KM process. The company wants to understand the dynamics of its KM model first, before it imposes exact measurements. Plus, Sequent believes that the interactions are too complex to offer a direct and indisputable causal link between KM and an item on the income statement. Indeed, imposing strident demands to cost-justify may misdirect efforts and miscommunicate purpose. In fact, the real business case is the cost of *not* getting the best information in the hands of sales teams.

The KM measure of the day: CONK or, the Cost of Not Knowing.

Hence the objective of Sequent's current measuring activities is to help inform and discipline KM practitioners so that they better relate their materials to the way the firm operates as a business. It does so by tracking variations in demand for knowledge and perceptions of cost and quality impact on its internal value chain. Recent employee surveys, in fact, reveal a growing perception of the utility and positive impact of SCEL and KM in general.

"This is not a search for the 'truth'," explains Swanson. "We are less interested in how knowledge is defined than in how its helps us. We want to focus on 'what works,' not on 'what is right.'"

TODAY AND INTO THE FUTURE

Something is certainly working right. Sequent is enjoying record revenue growth. According to the company's KM leaders, SCEL has helped Sequent raise project average selling price, and reduce delivery and response time at all stages in the sales and postsales process. It has also increased the amount of customer-specific and generic knowledge captured at the interface between the organization and downstream customers. SCEL has focused the sales teams more effectively on proper target markets and has made the assimilation process for new employees more efficient. Finally, the company has increased the customer-perceived value of its offerings, in hard (financial) and soft (loyalty) ways.

Just like any successful consumer products maker, Sequent intends to hone its product-development process through further insight into its knowledge customers' consumption patterns. "We are planning to do more monitoring," says Swanson. "Not from the big-brother perspective, but to gain knowledge on how to make information more useful for consumers."

Watch out for that "Big Brother" syndrome!

The company's future plans include:

- Regularly reviewing the design of the physical and logical structures of SCEL
- Providing better browsing structures that are generated automatically through the use of metadata
- Improving the security model to provide more control over who can access what
- Using SCEL as the front end for a variety of Web-enabled applications

Sequent also plans to extend the reach of KM outside its corporate walls. "We have distributors, suppliers, and manufacturing partners who could benefit greatly from SCEL," says Swanson. "Why not allow them access?" Obviously, there are security and competitive issues involved. "We're not sure how to do it yet," he says. Ultimately, however, the company believes it will gain more from sharing the most it can, than by revealing the least it must.

BUILDING THE "KNOWLEDGE ECONOMY"

Based on Sequent's experience with SCEL, Swanson offers the following key learnings:

1. *Look for the business linkage.* Think how knowledge can influence the world of its consumers: for instance, sales folks are motivated by faster close cycles.
2. *Business means not just revenue generation,* but also improving efficiency internally through best practice in operational processes.
3. *Technology is important.* However, since more and more applications are being developed with the Web technology in mind, KM managers need not be preoccupied with the migration and development of new KM/IT tools.
4. *Culture is very important.* But don't wait for the culture to change to start implementing knowledge networks. "Look for areas of interest and work with those who are interested," says Swanson.
5. *Start small and don't worry about the imperfections.* In many cases, "use itself converts the nonbelievers," he says.

Part Five

THE FOUR-PHASE PROCESS

OR "WHAT DO I DO ON MONDAY MORNING?"

We've come a long way.

In Part One we laid the foundation for internal transfer and told you how and why organizations leverage internal knowledge and best practices. In Part Two, we delved deeper into the value propositions to achieve dramatic improvements in customer intimacy, in operational excellence, and in product-to-market excellence. In Part Three, we described the enablers in detail. In Part Four, we added to our earlier wealth of examples by presenting four detailed cases of pioneers.

We've told you a great deal. But in a way, everything we've said is similar to telling a baby how it feels to be walking. It means very little until you take that first step. Part Five is all about how to take the first steps toward demonstrating the value of transfer. We will offer a simple four-phase process that could get your initial transfer projects off the ground quickly and successfully. We will give you more examples, especially from the World Bank and Amoco.

The following four-phase methodology can help organize the process of making best-practice transfer and knowledge sharing a mainstay of your company. This methodology (see the figure on p. 182) reflects the lessons learned from our APQC KM studies, and our own experience working with organizations to design knowledge management and transfer projects. One caveat: Every organization is different and the actual steps and issues in the methodology are never identical. The phases (plan, design, implement, and scale up) continue to hold true, but excellent diagnostic and change management skills are critical to meaningful design and execution.

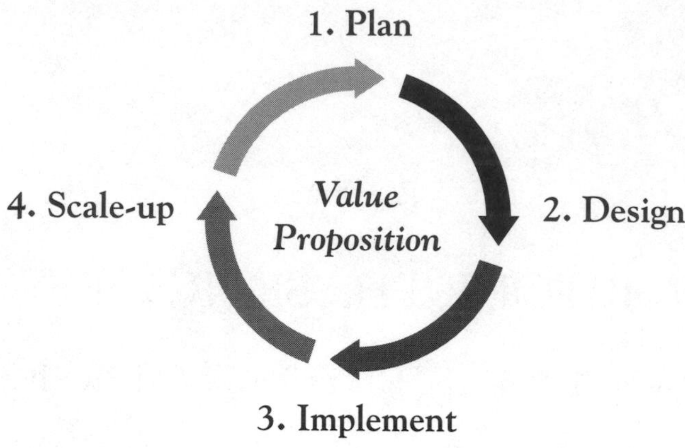

The Four-Phase Process

After all the "whys" and "whats," it's time for the "how-tos" of transfer. Knowledge without action is useless, and we want you to walk away from this book with a list actions that can advance and improve your organization's performance.

Chapter 18

PLAN, ASSESS, AND PREPARE

PHASE 1

"Plans are nothing: Planning is everything."
—Dwight D. Eisenhower

The objectives of phase 1 (typically led by a small task force or internal consulting group) include:

1. Assess your current opportunities for knowledge sharing
2. Discover your value proposition
3. Find a champion for the initial project(s)
4. Inform and prepare the organization
5. Define the business case

1. ASSESS YOUR CURRENT OPPORTUNITIES

How do you know where you're going if you don't know where you are?

Answer: You don't!

Hence, the first thing to do on "Monday morning" is to find out precisely where you are *today*—so you can figure out where you might be *tomorrow*.

There may be some areas of KM and best practice transfer where your company is already doing great. Other areas, however, may require serious work. Even companies that have not been formally practicing KM have initiatives underway that fit under its umbrella. Some of these early efforts may well serve as the foundation for an initial transfer project.

To get a quick size-up, answer these seven questions.

Question #1: *Do you know what knowledge you have now? Who has it? How can you get it, and—most critical!—which parts of it are truly valuable?* Few companies realize just how much knowledge they already have in the heads and files of their employees, or know where to find it and how to get it. Even fewer, however, understand how different "types" of knowledge can affect their performance. Recognizing the treasure chest of knowledge is the first step. Linking specific types of knowledge to the firm's value proposition (customer intimacy, product-to-market or operational excellence) is the second.

Question #2: *Do senior managers understand and support KM as a business strategy?* Many leaders don't understand that "knowledge" is an asset in which they must invest and which they can create, manage, and leverage. Others feel KM is but another fad. *If knowledge management is not hooked directly into the way business is managed and work gets done, it's not likely to go anywhere.*

Question #3: *Are you systematically transferring knowledge inside your organization?* Even if an organization realizes where it has that knowledge, it still does not mean valuable knowledge is systematically transferred from one part of the company to another—across departments, divisions, regions, the globe. Sometimes it isn't even transferred across the room!

Question #4: *Are you systematically acquiring outside knowledge? How? From whom? And is it being used?* Systematic acquisition of outside knowledge is frequently done through information searches, reverse engineering, competitive intelligence, and sales-force feedback. *Benchmarking* is another increasingly popular and powerful method. The latter involves finding, learning, and adapting best practices from someone who is doing the process better. Companies that rely on benchmarking often already have a sharing culture that encourages knowledge transfer and the implementation of best practices. *So if your answer to this query is a resounding "Yes," your organization most likely has even more knowledge to share.*

Question #5: *Are you leveraging knowledge as a product?* In your products? Leveraging knowledge as a product means selling your know-how and making money. The most famous example is American Airlines, which sells its travel know-how through its reservation system service, SABRE. Sears sells its logistic management expertise through its Sears Logistics subsidiary. IBM and Xerox have set up consulting services based on their knowledge. Management consulting firms are the ultimate example. They sell knowledge exclusively and entirely. *If you are set up to take knowledge and turn it into product/services, your organization is fulfilling the most important objective of KM: turning know-how into commercial value.*

Question #6: *Are you using technology to acquire, disseminate, and transfer knowledge? To everyone? Everywhere? Anytime?*

There are two errors you can make with technology investments in knowledge management: The first is to overinvest—in computers, software, modems, faxes, multimedia, cellular phones, video conferencing, personal communication systems, and the like. There is no question that these devices can assist knowledge transfer. They are almost essential. The danger is that you place technology ahead of the ability or the desire of people to use it. The second error is to underinvest and undermine your transfer initiatives. Naysayers say, "Wait!" fearing that a new technology will come along tomorrow. *If your organization has not linked its IT strategy to its KM and transfer strategy, it's got a long way to go.*

Question # 7: *Are you encouraging or discouraging knowledge sharing? Are people sharing? If not, why not?* In too many organizations, knowledge is not being shared for two reasons. First, sharing often runs counter to the culture. Until the culture is changed and incentives are created (more effective use of time, rewards, recognition, promotion), it's going to be difficult to get people to share. Second, most people aren't in the habit of sharing knowledge. The result is that valuable knowledge generated every day remains locked up in the minds of individuals throughout the organization. *If the organizational culture runs counter to sharing, you may be facing a tall—albeit not insurmountable—hurdle in implementing transfer initiatives.*

Obviously, answering seven questions is not a full assessment. We have found that a fuller assessment emerges while discovering your value proposition for transfer.

2. DISCOVER YOUR VALUE PROPOSITION

Finding the value proposition means answering this question: Where can knowledge management principles and tools have the greatest impact on strategic initiatives, projects, and processes? Usually a KM task force can find initial answers and direction through interviewing key players in the organization. Generally, the team's questions will resemble the following "to-do" task list:

Start with the business strategy:

- Revisit the organization's competitive strategy
- Identify key processes and "drivers" that affect the success of that strategy

Understand the current state:

- Which processes are suffering the most from knowledge gaps now?
- Are there projects underway now to address these processes? If the organization already is working on projects to support the value proposition, then perhaps these projects can be enhanced through the transfer of knowledge and best practices
- Understand the potential improvement (through internal and external benchmarking)
- Is there valuable knowledge, and information that could be converted to knowledge, that could enhance this process if it were accessible or used in a different manner?
- Assess, at a high level, the leadership and the cultural and technical landscape that will help or hinder a KM initiative

Develop a KM framework:

- Develop a conceptual model of how KM would help this process or project. You will use this framework to explain to people why transfer of knowledge and best practices could lead to better results.

Make realistic choices:

- Pick something (a project, process, or problem) that the leadership is committed to improving. Develop a value proposition of how KM would help.

MATCHING SYSTEM WITH VALUE

A KM/transfer strategy must match an organization's value proposition. At Buckman Laboratories, for instance, customer intimacy is a top revenue driver and a strategic imperative. So when the company embarked on its KM quest, it made sure its transfer projects were targeted at providing associates at the point of customer contact with instantaneous access to the collective IQ of the organization. "K'Netix," the resulting architecture, is a virtual "library" of the important information relevant to the business of the customer. The Knowledge Transfer Department (KTD)—a conglomeration of IS, telecommunications, and technical information center—is charged with:

- **Accelerating the accumulation and dissemination of knowledge within the company**
- **Providing easy and rapid access to the company's global knowledge bases**
- **Sharing best practices with all Buckman affiliates**

VALUE PROPOSITION PRINCIPLES FROM SEQUENT

- **Designers should start with the income statement, on Day 1, and work backwards into the design of the knowledge management infrastructure.**
- **Focus on a specific revenue-oriented pressure point (and its processes) within the firm's value chain.**
- **Think big, have good models, and talk about knowledge management internally, all the time, in practical language, using real-world examples that make sense to the people asked to participate in the system.**

3. FIND A CHAMPION

It is critical to find a champion or sponsor who (1) understands the need and (2) has the clout and resources to devote to supporting knowledge management and transfer initiatives. Based on the value proposition and the projects identified, it may be obvious who the champion(s) need to be. Without a powerful champion, the effort will probably stop here.

Once a champion has been found, the team can create a conceptual business case for the project or initiative. Then they can get the go-ahead to inform the organization, and resources to commence a design phase with a design team.

4. INFORM AND PREPARE THE ORGANIZATION

This task focuses on preparing the organization to understand the role of knowledge transfer and the project. The scale of this effort will depend on the scope of the project and how many people need to understand what is happening.

- Identify key stakeholder (internal customer) groups
- Articulate how they would benefit most from this project
- Inform and involve them
- Identify other successes already in your organization that resulted from more effective access to and sharing of knowledge to help build support and understanding

This information-exchange phase is by no means one-sided. By engaging in dialogue with key groups, you will be able to surface key issues and identify questions and barriers that will have to be addressed in designing your KM project.

5. DEFINE THE BUSINESS CASE

At this stage, the team should have a good picture of what projects, or transfer activities embedded in projects, will really support the value proposition; what results could be achieved and what it will cost in time and money. This allows them to define the business case for the project, create the business case, and get management approval and funding to proceed.

AMOCO'S APPROACH TO SHARED LEARNING

Amoco is an example of a KM work-in-process which illustrates the four-phase process and many of the enablers required to launch a transfer effort. We will use Amoco as an illustration of the four phases as they unfold.

In the early 1990s, Amoco's top management was engaged in organizational soul-searching. The goal was improving performance and reinvigorating the work force. The method was a fresh examination of the company's values. The result was a realization that continuous improvement is one of the values that is critical to the company's present and future success. The embodiment of this value was called Amoco Progress, or just "Progress" as it's known within the company—the corporate and personal commitment of everyone at Amoco to continuously improve.

The challenge for Amoco was developing a sustainable process that would foster ongoing learning and growth of its employees and its businesses. It needed a way to ensure that new and improved ways of doing work would permeate throughout the organization. Not occasionally. Not when there's a big push. But every day. And seamlessly.

This was no small task, considering the size and scope of Amoco's operations. One of the world's largest publicly traded diversified petrochemical companies, Amoco has about 42,000 employees in three sectors—Exploration & Production, Petroleum Products, and Chemicals, in multiple locations all over the world.

To get its intellectual arms around the potential payoff of sharing, as well as the organizational elements required to make it work, Amoco set up a task force in 1994. This "Shared Learning" team was an ad hoc group of employees recruited from across the company. Members were handed two mandates: First, examine the potential results of sharing effective practices and knowledge. Second, examine the necessary support systems (i.e., enablers) and structure that would make transfer of knowledge and effective practices possible.

Meanwhile, on a less formalized basis, networks of experts and communities of practice throughout Amoco agreed to make this issue one of their key focuses as well. "It was the beginning of a great speeding-up of learning across all of Amoco," says Bill Lowrie, president of Amoco and executive sponsor for Shared Learning.

The plan the Amoco task force presented to management will be described in the next chapter.

Chapter 19

DESIGNING THE TRANSFER PROJECT

PHASE 2

The objectives of the design phase are:

1. Decide the scale of the initiative
2. Use the learnings from others in "best practices in design"
3. Create the action plan and marshal all the resources (including technologies, people, and communications)

1. DETERMINE THE SCALE OF THE INITIATIVE

We begin with the assumption that *eventually* you will want to embed the transfer of knowledge and best practices into the fabric of your organization (including the appropriate enablers: culture, information technology, infrastructure, and measurement). But you've got to start somewhere. And you ought to start somewhere that's manageable.

The only thing worse than deciding not to do anything is deciding to do everything at once and failing *to show any success or results within a reasonable time frame*.

THINK BIG, START SMALL

At the outset of this new effort, you must decide how grand your initial plan and scope need to be. There are two ways you could go: Start with projects and learn from them, always keeping in mind the ultimate objective and need for an integrated approach; or alternatively, design a grand plan and infrastructure from the start, and roll it out gradually.

Our KM study participants spanned the spectrum in their initial scope (see How They Started, below). Some began by applying KM and best-practice transfer projects to a *specific need or project*, as Texas Instruments did with its Wafer Fabrication initiative, and expanded from there. At Monsanto, for example, initial success in Ceregen, a pharmaceutical division, provided the compelling business case for organization-wide rollout. National Semiconductor began its transfer of knowledge and best practices work as a grass-roots effort that is just now getting renewed through top-level support.

Others, like Sequent, Buckman, and Arthur Andersen, took the "*Grand Plan*" approach. They began years ago by creating a company-wide architecture and sharing capability and improved it with experience. Arthur Andersen's KM architecture has changed and evolved over a five-year period, but AA has had a firmwide knowledge capture and sharing intention from the beginning. Still others, like CIGNA Property & Casualty, used KM principles to complement enterprise-wide reengineering work.

So, from a practical standpoint, the answer to "Where do I start? " depends on the firm's KM readiness (indicated by the self-assessment); what the business need is (radical improvement now, or steady move up the curve?); how much buy-in exists into the KM concept at the top echelons; available resources; and how much infrastructure can realistically be created to support the initiative.

BIGGER MAY NOT BE BETTER

Even when the resources and management buy-in are present, we still recommend starting with a scalable project and a flexible overall design.

Why?

First, a "grand design" may be too restrictive for a field that is only now evolving. "I do not know if any of the alternatives constitute the *right* model," writes Onno van Ewyk, of HCI consulting in Sydney, Australia. "There is a danger in choosing a model at this stage in that it encourages managers to try to construct what looks like the right thing without attending properly to any of the underlying dynamics," van

Ewyk continues. "Ultimately, successful business is a performance art and the players are always the organization's people (whether the people are employees or operating in some other form of relationship). Knowledge management can only ever be a means of enhancing and supporting their performance. If an organization develops KM with this in mind then the right model will emerge."

Second, such "grand scheme" may prove too overwhelming—unnecessarily. Such models or designs are never "entirely" executed. Spending lots of time initially (instead of actually doing the work of transfer and sharing) may lead to paralysis and delay the "good work." Says Karl Erik Sveiby, noted KM expert: "Do not try to create a '*Knowledge Organization*,' or any other kind of 'organization' for that matter, because models are always unrealistic. They are, at best, approximate representations of their designer's tacit knowledge. Try to 'see' instead, by using these concepts as a language for dialogue and treat the suggested performance indicators as vision enhancing devices."

In contrast, there are big benefits to beginning with "chewable" chunks of projects:

- A project provides early evidence of value.
- Projects allow learning and experimentation on a small, manageable scale.
- Projects help the organization to understand the IT requirements.
- Projects reveal the change management issues:
  - The role of champion and sponsor
  - The criteria for appropriate projects
  - They build experienced and credible advocates
  - They identify the required resources
- The design team learns how to learn, how to observe, what to watch for, and what matters and what doesn't.
- Finally, projects teach you lessons for future scale-up to the Grand Plan.

2. BEST PRACTICES IN DESIGN

Whereas designing a KM or transfer project is different from, say, a reengineering project, some tried-and-true *design guidelines* apply across many projects. They include the following:

A CHECKLIST FOR CHOOSING THE "RIGHT" PROJECT

1. ***Select projects that advance your business performance.*** Don't do "KM" projects. Projects must meet business needs in both appearance and practice. Depending on your firm's value proposition, project objectives might be:

- Reduce cycle times
- Reduce cost
- Enhance product development and innovation
- Increase reuse and efficiency

2. ***Select projects that have a high probability of success.*** Particularly for your first efforts, you want early and clear success stories to help validate and propagate the cause of knowledge sharing. How can you tell which one's a likely winner?

- Can you articulate how knowledge management will contribute?
- What is the business importance outside the immediate user community?
- How strong is the business case?
- Is the project funded?
- Is senior management willing to champion the project?
- What's the risk associated with failure (as relates to business criticality)?
- Is the implementation scalable?

3. ***Select projects which are appropriate for exploring emerging technologies.*** This will give you a head-start on the scale-up while reducing

- Form a multidisciplinary design team of users, technology experts, and change facilitators. It takes this kind of team to address all the important issues in a project of any significance.
- Ensure the design team learns as much as possible about knowledge management applications, barriers, and approaches, and how others have addressed them. Draw on the experience and knowledge of other knowledge management practitioners.
- Design the IT support backward from the business issue and objective; don't start with the technology.
- Address the change management questions.
- Identify how this project will help people do their jobs better.

later anxiety about new systems and ways of doing work. To choose the right IT for your project, assess the following:

- **What's the degree of passion, commitment, and comfort of users with ambiguity and chaos (trial and error)?**
- **Does the project provide the necessary attraction ("rush," reward) that will enable the user community to sustain themselves through the change?**
- **Is the entire culture (user, management, etc.) compatible with the approach required?**
- **If we don't apply the emerging technology (KM) now, how difficult would it be to retrofit?**

4. *Select projects which have significant potential for building credibility for knowledge and best practice transfer as a discipline within the organization.* To make the right choice, ask the following questions:

- **What is the potential reusability of captured knowledge beyond the primary audience?**
- **What is the potential for learnings from this project to be used as a template/blueprint for future projects?**
- **Does the process itself require high amounts of knowledge, skills, experience, and expertise?**
- **How will this project help us broaden the depth and the breadth of our use and understanding of knowledge management?**
- **Will the people involved in this project be able to help evolve our culture toward one that is more "knowledge management friendly"?**

- Create common standards for information technology infrastructure.
- Develop an approach to capture and learn from your experiences, and decide how that knowledge will be shared.
- Revisit the objectives and change management strategy constantly, as the action plan takes shape.

3. CREATE THE PROJECT PLAN

Once developed, a project action plan will include the following information:

1. Key milestones and phases/steps
2. How to involve others
   - Whose involvement and buy-in are critical to success?
3. How to communicate and educate
   - How to share lessons learned and proposed approach
   - How to educate and train those who need to support this effort
4. Resources and budget
5. Assigned "owner(s)" for each major component or deliverable from the design

IT DESIGN QUESTIONS

An information technology approach must be designed to reflect the overall project design and approach. IT should not drive the design, although it will create constraints on what can be done now, while taking into account future scalability and cross-enterprise compatibility.

The following are some of the questions that need to be addressed during the design phase regarding the use of information technology:

***Content:* What is the nature of the content (information or knowledge) that will be involved? How will it be used or shared? Different applications are appropriate for different content. Some applications are, by their nature, organization-wide. Customer databases are an example. Others, such as discussion forums, may only affect the people in the community of practice, or project team using the forum.**

***Audience:* Who will be using the content or participating in the process? How? How does this fit the way they work now?**

***Access and platform:* What technology platform will have the greatest ease of use and scalability for the future? Are off-the-shelf applications available? Legacy systems and stand-alone databases present a challenge.**

***Use and interaction:* How will the content be captured and refreshed? How will quality be addressed? What are the norms of behavior? Are any policies required?**

***People and roles:* What support roles and people will be needed to ensure results? This includes technology support, facilitators, coaches, and information resources. (See Chapter 11 on infrastructure and facilitators.)**

THE DESIGN PHASE IN AMOCO

By November 1995, Amoco's strategic planning committee accepted the recommendations from the Shared Learning team, including:

1. Set expectations for the capture, transfer, and use of learnings and best practices across the organization and from external sources. Establish the strategic importance of doing so to improve business.
   - Define key strategic areas/processes where best practices should be identified and used throughout the organization.
   - Make the transfer of learnings and best practices a part of business strategy and develop annual performance plans to identify and close performance gaps
   - Assess progress in this area through milestones related to closing performance gaps, such as the achievement of defined benchmarks and other stretch targets, through the ongoing monitoring of metrics related to the capture, transfer, and use of processes, and through insights gained and improvements achieved through the Amoco business assessment process.
   - Develop plans to overcome identified barriers to implementing the recommendations of this study in their organizations.
2. Make a computer system available worldwide for storing and retrieving learnings and practices, and manage the system to provide the best available learnings and practices wherever and whenever needed.
3. Define, encourage, support, and manage competency networks in key strategic functional areas that can leverage knowledge, and assist in managing the knowledge capture and transfer processes. These networks should be well publicized and given responsibility for providing "experts-on-call" services.
4. Incorporate effective learning/sharing behaviors and competencies into the Leadership Development Process, the Performance Benchmarks of the Amoco Performance Management System, and into Leadership and Progress-related training. Promote awareness of the many successful approaches that have been used within

and outside Amoco for the capture, transfer, and use of best practices.

5. Promote corporatewide recognition of individuals, teams, and organizations who are role models of capturing, sharing, and using learnings and best practices.
6. Commit additional resources at the corporate, business group, and local levels to support implementation of the above recommendations, in particular to create and manage the knowledge capture, transfer, and use processes, and to further develop Amoco's capabilities in these areas.

Based on these recommendations, the Amoco Steering Committee launched its early projects in knowledge sharing and transfer and created a corporate infrastructure to support those projects. They moved quickly to implementation, as illustrated in the next chapter (see page 205).

Chapter 20

IMPLEMENTATION

PHASE 3

The objectives of this third phase are action-oriented:

1. Launch the project
2. Provide support for both content and process
3. Observe and learn
4. Achieve results

The seeds of a successful implementation are sown in the first two phases. If you have a compelling value proposition and clear business case, a passionate champion and a culture bent on sharing, adequate resources and a realistic plan—then implementation involves taking the plan off the paper and into the trenches. It's about turning "knowledge" into action.

It's also probably the toughest phase of the process because you will find—as many have—the best plans falter in the face of day-to-day realities. To survive and excel, remember this: Keep your plan *flexible* and adjust it constantly to emerging circumstances and oscillating emotions. And they *will* oscillate.

1. LAUNCH THE PROJECT

Just how to implement a transfer project will be determined by the particular project and the type of knowledge and practices being transferred. The following are four prototypical projects.

1. *Learning from prior/new product launches*. For example, if the transfer project is to capture and use lessons learned from prior new product launches, implementation would focus on bringing the teams and individuals with past experience together with those who are part of the new product launch team. Initial meetings or conversations would revolve around what worked and what didn't, how past experiences relate to the current initiative, what is different and what can be adapted, and what should be stored in a database as "universal knowledge" valuable enough to be stored in the organization's long-term memory.

2. *Improving operational performance*. If the project is intended to identify and transfer best practices between similar operations, the approach that often works best is forming cross-unit best practice teams, composed of "experts" from the disparate locations. The teams go through natural phases, and need facilitation at each phase: (1) identifying what they really mean by the process and creating a shared vocabulary (i.e., scoping and mapping the process); (2) identifying current practice; (3) comparing performance to identify best practices; and (4) adapting and implementing. Facilitators will be required to help the teams throughout the process, then coach and monitor implementation.

3. *Reusing designs*. If the project's goal is to capture historical information or engineering designs that can be reused, then the implementation challenge is far different. The *planning* and *design* phases would have identified the types and nature of knowledge that must be captured and codified, as well as the correct IT infrastructure to allow the knowledge to be reused. But "theoretical" design—even the best sort—is radically different from cajoling and training people to actually work differently by getting others' designs, and getting their consent that indeed, the effort (to change) is worth it. Again, the seeds for success must be sown during the earlier phases. If there is a champion with enough clout and a compelling business need, then the odds are greater that people will go through the discomfort and frustration of changing the way they work.

4. *Building communities of practice*. If the objective of the project is to create ongoing networks of likeminded people or communities of prac-

tice, then facilitators again play a key role in bringing people together across functions and locations. It will be the role of facilitators to help participants set objectives and learn to communicate and learn from each other: This "learning-to-learn" process is the most critical part of implementing a network-oriented transfer effort.

2. PROVIDE SUPPORT

No matter how "specific" the objective or effort, and whether it's designed to improve product development or increase operational excellence, some "basic" truisms run through most implementation phases:

1. *Face-to-face is critical—at the outset.* Early "knowledge" exchanges involve a wealth of tacit knowledge. Consequently, it's not enough to simply have a "historian" meet with the "past" teams to "record" what they've learned. Recording is a pale and wholly inadequate imitation of the kind of dynamics and problem-driven questions that a new team is likely to ask if they are in a dialogue with the more experienced crew. So let them meet, and interact, if you want to ensure your implementation phase gets off on the right foot.

2. *A one-shot deal is never good enough.* "Old" and "new" teams—or simply teams from various sides of the organization—will need to have ongoing access to each other, in order to confront new issues and address problems as they arise. A one-shot "recording" session or even a one-shot face-to-face meeting is unlikely to achieve long-term success. To guarantee the effort remains an iterative process, build in constant access and interaction.

3. *Facilitators will earn their "money's worth."* No matter whether the implementation process involves different functional groups, or similar groups but at disparate locations, it helps to have a champion or facilitator present to bridge attitudes, vocabulary, and knowledge gaps. A need for "brokers" has been driving the spectacular growth in the management consulting business. It's a lot easier to hear criticism and new ideas if you do not perceive the "conveyer" as a threat. Plus, every process needs a "master," or at least a "nurturer," to make sure it does not fade into corporate oblivion. Designate internal "consultants" who

are respected by employees or have a natural inclination to "bridge" to help keep your implementation process on track.

4. *Do everything possible to achieve early, visible results.* The attention span of today's organizations is shorter than ever, because the demands

BUCKMAN LABORATORIES LAUNCH "AIDS"

Bob Buckman, vice-chairman of Buckman Laboratories, was the key architect of the original design for their knowledge management and information technology system. Buckman realized in implementing the knowledge sharing culture that it would not be easy to get all associates motivated and involved. He offers the following tips.

Make it fun. On-line contests can be used to increase involvement. Buckman has a Notice Board Section, called Breakroom, where all associates go to ask questions on a wide range of social topics, e.g., items for sale or wanted, requests for a good local home-maintenance professional, interesting restaurants, helpful tips in arranging a foreign vacation, any item of personal interest that does not violate the Code of Ethics.

Lessen the stress. Buckman employees were allowed to access the system in a more relaxed environment, such as from their homes.

Nominate captains. At Buckman, two experts in each forum were appointed to play the role of "answer-givers."

Get all associates on the system. With involvement of all associates, the risk of losing untapped resources is minimized.

Renew the passport. Implement the system on a global basis so that all cultures are comfortable and maintain involvement.

Provide functionality as well as portability. Because of global operations, traveling staff need computer "survival kits." These are signed out based on a specific country and contain adapters, cords, and other peripheral accessories.

Make it easy. The change is difficult enough so it must be made as easy and user-friendly as possible. K'Netix operates in a Windows environment and was designed to be both intuitive and flexible.

Provide training. Informal training, intensive training, and ongoing training help with the transition. At Buckman, documentation is provided in the form of a K'Netix training/reference manual.

Monitor progress. By whatever factor(s) indicate success in a given system, that progress should be documented.

are constantly changing. It is critical that projects selected for these early transfer and KM pilots show visible results within at most six months.

IMPLEMENTATION AT CHEVRON

In 1992, with a corporate imperative to cut costs (the value proposition), Chevron set up thirteen best practice teams composed of refinery managers, operations personnel, best practice study personnel, and volunteers. Together, the teams set out to examine "hard refinery processes" like crude distillation, as well as corporatewide processes such as energy efficiency and conservation; their ultimate goal was to identify the "best" ones and then help others within the organization implement the best practices. The teams' initial focus was on areas where improvement could yield short-term, high-value results.

Indeed, according to Jim O'Brient, manager of quality improvement in Chevron's USA production company, it should take *no more* than six to twelve months to achieve some success and gain credibility.

Projected results from each project ranged from $10 million in savings to $150 million. Front-loading success—and picking improvements that can yield visible change within a reasonable time—have been critical to building overall credibility and facilitating later scale-up.

By the end of the first year, the energy efficiency team generated $150 million in initial savings; by 1997, they had achieved a total savings of $648 million, by both following a model that takes each initial "saving idea" and scaling it up across Chevron for greater results. The gas compression team created $20 million in sustainable first-year improvements on a $500,000 investment (mostly people's time).

Similarly, Chevron has taken the initial thirteen teams and scaled them up to help ignite change enterprisewide. Teams are focused on specific business areas. Their work is credited with improving everything from catalytic cracking to plant maintenance. Each team meets three to four times a year and sets aside time to share ideas and lessons learned, as well as categorize knowledge into various levels of "applicability" from good ideas to best practices.

To keep the improvement and transfer work on track, Chevron has been relying on "experts" and "process masters." These professional facilitators are charged with providing continuity and keeping the process moving as well as ensuring project goals and business goals remain intimately linked.

The focus on best practice transfer continues to spread in Chevron. For example, Chevron spends nearly $6 billion a year on capital projects. In 1991, they benchmarked the best practices of sixty-plus companies and developed a world-class project planning and management process. The task then became deploying the best practices methodology, known as the Chevron Project Development and Execution Process process, to all the capital projects in Chevron. All the lessons learned from earlier transfer work have supported this effort. The CPDEP ("chip dip") network of best practices in capital projects has made a dramatic difference in project management timelines and costs at Chevron. There has been over $816 million in savings in downstream capital projects since 1992. Adding this to other savings, Chevron has reduced its annual operating expense by over $1.5 billion since 1992. On top of all the savings, Chevron is creating a culture that values learning from others as a source of competitive advantage.

BRITISH PETROLEUM

In 1994, British Petroleum Exploration (BPX) launched a "virtual teamwork program." The project was designed to create effective ways for members of teams to collaborate across different locations. The goal: building a *network of people*, not a *storehouse of data*, information, or knowledge.

BPX realized that with the level and wealth of technical expertise within its organization, it would be far more efficient to give employees access to other employees' tacit knowledge than to capture and codify that knowledge electronically or on paper.

To get the process rolling, BPX's "Change Management Team" (the design and implementation team) developed a coaching program to show participants how to use the technology (when necessary) as well as help them understand how reaching out to others could further their work. The company decided to call the implementation help "coaching," not "training," to ensure it retains a touch of personal interaction like a coach working with players rather than a trainer presenting information to passive recipients. The coaching curriculum included not only the "how to," but "why" and "what." About half the budget was spent on coaching. After the pilot project was completed, the Change Management Team was reincarnated as the Knowledge Management Team, responsible for roll-out across BP (the eventual scale-up).

AMOCO'S "FAST" IMPLEMENTATION

In February 1996, Amoco appointed Dave Ledet the director of Shared Learning, and he began formal implementation. When the company announced Ledet's new role, Vice President of Progress Don Tornberg sent a letter to leaders of all Amoco's business groups and units asking them to use the Shared Learning Study as a guide to accelerating transfer of knowledge across the company. It was clear that Ledet and Shared Learning had support from the top.

Befitting a large-scale change initiative, "implementation" involved a clear understanding and ongoing management of what Amoco identified as the four key enablers of successful Shared Learning—focus, alignment, support, and time (FAST).

Focus helps people determine what knowledge should be captured and transferred. It is critical to successful Shared Learning because it allows people to see a clear reason for this activity. Many groups at Amoco focus their Shared Learning efforts on elements of their business strategy. "Focus is relatively easy at a local level," Ledet says. "Organizations know what they want to accomplish, whether that's growth or process improvement. What gets a little harder is determining focus for sharing across internal organizations, but that is where you break down boundaries and get the best benefits out of shared learning."

At Amoco, *alignment* involves the cultural and performance metrics that help match individuals' goals to those of the company. Instead of issuing a corporate mandate (push) to share, Amoco focused on generating demand (pull) for Shared Learning by raising employee awareness of it; shifting the company culture to make Shared Learning an expected, normal part of work; and embedding it into Amoco's processes. Ledet and his team dedicate significant time to working with key personnel around the world, including corporate leaders whose concerns and whose public and private speeches often set a pace for the company. Other channels leveraged to generate demand for Shared Learning include newsletters, e-mail bulletins, demonstrations at internal conferences and meetings, and an intranet site. Ledet and his staff are also pursuing alignment by working with Human Resources to include Shared Learning as an element in the company's standard performance review processes.

"People don't do this because we're 'dangling a carrot' in front of them. They do it because it fundamentally makes sense to them that we need to know what we know. It makes sense that we need to develop new knowledge," says Ledet. "The only way to make learning systemic in the organization is by integrating learning principles into processes, such as project management or strategic planning."

To *support* its people's efforts to share, Amoco provides coaching, tools, and processes in a wide range of areas, including developing a change management framework, training in Shared Learning, and developing and using database applications. "Once people are ready to try knowledge management, you must be ready with resources to help them," Ledet says. "Otherwise, they hit a dead end. If that's allowed to happen, it takes five times the effort to get them to try again."

Infrastructure support is guided by a corporate-level change management team of two: Ledet and Julie Greer, progress consultant. A battalion of change agents in every Amoco business unit bolster the effort on the front lines. These quality/progress professionals help employees make their Shared Learning processes work on a local level. They spread the word. They answer questions. They make sure employees have access to tools.

The other element of the infrastructure support picture is technological systems. In the original Shared Learning study, Amoco identified Lotus Notes as the most appropriate tool for developing a corporation-wide repository of knowledge. The original format developed for the database has been reused many times by special interest groups around the company. To find the information they needed, users accessed a knowledge resource Index (KRI) which listed knowledge sharing forums, such as databases, communities of interest, expertise lists, meetings, internal web sites, and others by topic. The next-generation navigation tool—incorporating intranet technology—allowed users not only to search for resources on a particular subject but also to access them directly through the navigation tool/browser. Amoco is using Lotus Notes and Domino to make interactive knowledge sharing databases available to everyone via the Netscape browser.

Employees may see the value and have the systems and training to facilitate sharing, but more often than not, they don't have the *time*. "While we all recognize that learning ultimately results in a net savings in time and work, fighting the alligators often takes precedence over draining the swamp," according to Ledet. To ensure employees set aside time for sharing knowledge, Amoco has been promoting regular meetings of communities of practice. It has also emphasized that those who share will be recognized. For example, success stories from the front lines were shared at a May 1997 global Amoco conference, topped by a presentation of the Chairman's Award for Excellence to fifty teams best using applied Amoco progress principles for superior business results.

Chapter 21

TRANSITION AND SCALE-UP

PHASE 4

The objectives of this phase are to:

1. Capture success stories and publicize early results
2. Use knowledge gained to expand the scale-up
3. Create a new organizational structure to oversee the ongoing process

1. CAPTURE SUCCESS STORIES AND PUBLICIZE EARLY RESULTS

You've done it! You found the right project, identified the value proposition, designed a realistic plan, and implemented your first transfer project. And it works!

Now what? Now, it's time to figure out how to harness the engine of KM and best practice transfer to turbo-power your entire organization.

The first order of business is leveraging the experiential knowledge you've already got. It is important to have a record of early successes, and elaborate anecdotal examples and testimonials about the contribution of knowledge management to the business results, so:

- Capture success stories; they can be used for learning and "selling."
- Identify and list lessons learned.
- Codify the first good experience—and enlist the participants as missionaries and coaches for future projects.

Then:

- Use lessons learned to create an expansion and scale-up strategy.
- Identify the entity that will guide, support, and monitor KM on an organization-wide basis.

It is the explicit need/inclination to observe, learn, and capitalize on existing know-how that sets KM and best practice transfer apart from other improvement projects. Hence, throughout the early stages, both facilitators and participants must capture and transfer learnings about the process of design and implementation so they can (1) enhance the organization's core competency at transfer, and (2) prepare for scale-up—expanding the process to other topics and constituencies.

2. USE KNOWLEDGE GAINED TO EXPAND THE SCALE-UP

We've used the example of *Texas Instruments* throughout this book. We go back to it here because we believe that what makes TI's best-practice transfer effort sustainable is the conscious effort to learn from initial tryouts and apply these learnings to ongoing scale-up initiatives.

For example, during the assessment phase of TI's first year of transfer work—the "*year of supply*" as TI has dubbed it—the organization's best practice commando teams not only identified "best practices"; they also identified gaps and strengths in the company's efforts to share. Both the gaps (need to do better or know more) and strengths were documented by best practice facilitators. The knowledge captured during the first year led to the "*year of demand*"—the second phase of the organization-wide program which involved a massive cultural change initiative aimed at creating a demand for solutions to gaps identified earlier.

At *Buckman Laboratories*, the vision of a full-scale effort, a way of connecting associates with powerful knowledge bases, existed from day one. Even so, Buckman started with a pilot project, focused on the sales people, and only then scaled up. Now all 1,200 employees have laptops and CompuServe accounts.

3. CREATE NEW ORGANIZATIONAL STRUCTURES

In many cases, the scale-up stage also requires the formation of a new organizational entity. A pilot project can possibly be managed part time, or by a makeshift team of temporary facilitators. However, if you intend to embed KM and transfer into the core of your operations, and expand their reach enterprise-wide, the human/organizational infrastructure must be institutionalized to ensure continuity and focus.

- At *Buckman*, the scale-up led to the merger of IT and KM into the Knowledge Transfer System (KTS) department which is currently charged with managing all aspects of KM within Buckman.
- At *Texas Instruments*, early successes led to the formation of the TI Office of Best Practices, which has two functions: (1) it defines the best practice sharing process, facilitator and champion roles, as well as technology infrastructure for sharing; and (2) it is the engine for developing and deploying training and infrastructure supported by the facilitator network and sharing process.

SEQUENT'S GUIDE TO IMPLEMENTATION AND SCALE-UP

Originally focused mostly on marketing and sales, Sequent Computers took the following steps during design and implementation to support eventual scale-up:

Start by providing a common space for storing and retrieving knowledge and having discussions. Then, examine what people use, what they contribute to, and immediate feedback they give to redesign the system. Look at trend patterns of use. Then, begin to engineer more sophisticated social expectations about use. Finally, roll the system out to more people and design new releases that incorporate learning from initial experiences.

SUMMARY: THE "SCALER-UPPER" ACTION LIST

When it's time to shift from small-scale to full-scale, most organizations will need both to address learnings from the pilot and to prepare the organization for scale-up. Some of these "preparatory" actions might include:

1. Providing a forum for lessons learned and information sharing/collaboration on existing projects and initiatives that involve KM principles
2. Reviewing and adjusting (if necessary) corporate reward and recognition programs, including incentive compensation, to focus attention on knowledge sharing with the goal of achieving business objectives
3. Developing a means/process for advertising business and technology initiatives that focus on the collection and sharing of customer and employee information to reduce or eliminate redundant efforts
4. Reviewing and adjusting corporate and business systems to enable collaboration and communication within and among business groups
5. Designating a function to coordinate and maintain focus on knowledge sharing to achieve corporate objectives

---

AMOCO'S TIME TO SCALE UP

Throughout 1996–97, Amoco made great strides in creating a culture of Shared Learning. "My sense is that when we started to do this people weren't sure what we wanted to do or that it was okay to do it," according to Dave Ledet. "Although over 500 people were involved in building the Shared Learning strategy, in retrospect, we should have involved more to build commitment. Still, by getting Shared Learning in front of employees and facilitating some successes around the company we were creating an environment where people see Shared Learning is something they need—and are expected—to do. Just as it is expected that we show up at a certain time in the morning, it's expected that we share our knowledge."

With the basic concepts in place, Ledet and his Shared Learning team are working to enable the change to be integrated deeper into the organization. While some groups within Amoco are sharing their learnings instinctively, some have only taken the first steps to developing a formalized change plan within their own groups. A systematic, process-focused approach to Shared Learning is what is needed to capture the maximum benefits, and cause the corporation to think and act as one. While Amoco has realized significant benefits and improvements due to their Shared Learning implementation (below), there is still a lot of improvement left to accomplish.

IS IT WORKING AT AMOCO?

Evidence #1. In the Norwegian North Sea area, Amoco drilling operations personnel recently had to quickly decide how to fix a crippling problem with an operating well. Using a company-wide synthesis of best practices in drilling, the team coordinated the complex work in only one day. Without access to shared knowledge, the same project would have taken five to ten days—at least.

Evidence #2. In Texas City, Texas, crews at the Amoco refinery are using hand-held computer technology transferred from a plant in Wyoming— yielding hundreds of thousands of dollars in working capital gains through avoided equipment failures, increased run times, and reduced maintenance costs.

Evidence #3. At Richard Elsenheimer's office in the Amoco Chemicals plant outside Alvin, Texas, the phone is ringing off the hook. Since Elsenheimer spoke at a Community of Interest (COI) meeting of Amoco maintenance managers last year, a steady stream of maintenance personnel from around the country have been calling him to learn what his team has done and to cooperate for mutual gain.

Evidence #4. While planning the Purified Terephthalic Acid (PTA) plant in Geel, Belgium, the team learned from other PTA projects at Amoco, applied the learnings, and reduced the overall project cost by 10 percent from the original estimate. They also applied new technology that recovers energy from the process to allow the plant to actually produce and export electrical power, and to significantly reduce waste water treatment loads by recycling the solvent stream.

Evidence #5. The Trinidad Upstream Development Project provides for onshore and offshore facilities to produce 550 million standard cubic feet of gas daily for a liquified natural-gas plant on the West Coast of Trinidad. This project team also learned from other project teams around Amoco, and applied a novel contracting strategy. They formed a true partnership with six contractors and involved them early in the project, for an estimated saving over the life of the project of $85 million. The performance contracts allowed all of the members of the partnership or alliance to make additional profits by realizing a high level of performance.

Evidence #6. The Marlin project is Amoco's initial step into deepwater Gulf of Mexico, a $500 million tension leg platform (TLP) drilling in over 3,200 feet of water. The team also used learnings from other parts of Amoco and external companies to develop the project. As a result of prior experience, they decided to have two separate engineering firms develop different designs concurrently and then picked one to go forward with. The cost of the additional unused design was far outweighed by the cycle time saved, and the increased project efficiency, both in design and construction. The overall estimated savings for the project are $20 million.

In addition to these results, Amoco is also measuring progress on knowledge sharing on a more formalized basis. The primary measure is an annual survey which gauges, among other things, awareness of the Shared Learning concept and employees' application of it. "Basically, about 60 percent of people in our company favorably respond to questions like 'Are you capturing and transferring your best practices?' 'Are you using effective practices from other organizations?'" Ledet reported in 1997.

Ledet spends a good amount of time gathering more informal feedback. Most Amoco managers tell Ledet that they know Shared Learning is working when they see people applying lessons learned from others. Amoco also collects activity measures, such as how often Shared Learning databases are used. Nonetheless, most of the data gathered is about project-specific reports on the success of Shared

Learning. Many of these do involve hard financial results. For example, Amoco drilling operations expects to save $50 million a year through Shared Learning.

Amoco's Levels of Knowledge

Earlier we outlined the way AMP, TI, and Chevron define the "best" in best practice (see What Does "Best Practices" Mean Anyway? on page 12). To make its burgeoning community of databases easier to manage, Amoco also developed a multilayered approach that categorizes experience and practice into three levels:

1. Tier I, or the "innovative knowledge level," has the lowest degree of structure and minimal criteria for material entered. The goal is to allow users to freely input their experiences, successes, lessons learned, or requests for information. Quality of the material input varies, but by maximizing the amount of input the potential for collaboration and virtual learning is also maximized.
2. The next level of the taxonomy is Tier II, or "proven knowledge." Data at this level can be the result of collaboration on Tier I. Although it may not have corporate-wide application, the transfer of information at this level has proven value. It is also more structured and meets criteria for inclusion. Tier II Shared Learnings include local methodologies, policies and procedures, emerging best practices, success stories, effective performance measures, and lessons learned. However, the structure is still flexible enough to encourage further collaboration and growth of knowledge capital. At this tier, collaboration enables identification of best knowledge, including some industry best practices.
3. Tier III is "best knowledge." This is where the company's "secrets of success" will reside, including methodologies, best practices, core competencies, policies, and values. Information at this level requires highest-level approval and rigorous screening.

THE FOUR PHASES IN ACTION AT THE WORLD BANK

In October 1996, World Bank President James Wolfensohn announced at its annual meeting that the World Bank planned to capture and organize its experience and know-how and make it available not only to internal staff but also to clients, partners, and stakeholders around the world. The World Bank was to become "the Knowledge Bank," with substantial transformation of the international organization which aims at reducing poverty and improving the quality of life in developing countries through lending and advisory services.

Using Stories to Drum Up Support

Introducing knowledge management was a significant challenge. At the time, there were some pilot efforts under way in several areas, including the education sector, private sector infrastructure, and the live data base in Africa. These efforts were perceived as successful and helped make the case for introducing the approach more widely across the organization. Many other key elements were missing. There was little agreement on the strategy for knowledge management, and there was no budget or institutional decision-making mechanism for knowledge management, and no way of tracking or monitoring activities.

In mid-October 1996, Stephen Denning was appointed program director, Knowledge Management in the World Bank to help introduce knowledge management on an institution-wide basis. A year later, the main elements for implementation were in place. Knowledge management would be part of a strategic compact that was unanimously approved by the board of executive directors in March 1997. A substantial budget for fiscal year 1998 was passed and put in place. The Bank established an institutional decision-making mechanism with two representative forums—the Information and Knowledge Management Council and the Knowledge Management Board. They also now had a method for tracking and monitoring the progress of implementing knowledge management in the Bank.

The use of stories was a key element in explaining the concept of knowledge management. Stories were more effective than charts, or reports. Dialogue was effective but difficult to use for large numbers of managers and employees.

An early powerful story was that of a task team in a Latin American country. The client country wanted quickly the Bank's global experience of the policy and political implications of education reform. The Bank's task team contacted the help desk of the Education Network, who quickly obtained the relevant material from the relevant community of practice. The task team was able to meet the client's needs more quickly and completely than they otherwise would. This in itself was an accomplishment, but knowledge management takes the process further. The material that was developed in this engagement has now been identified as "valuable knowledge objects" to be edited for inclusion in the Bank's electronic knowledge base so that they can be instantly accessed by anyone else in the organization. When the Bank's knowledge base goes external, the materials—suitably edited—will be instantly available to clients and partners and stakeholders around the world, thus enormously expanding and accelerating the reach of the Bank's know-how and expertise to groups that would otherwise not have access.

Complex system ideas like this could be communicated effectively and widely in this story format, whereas efforts to explain them in charts, or reports, often ran into difficulties.

Denning found that stories work because they are efficient "carriers" of high-impact tacit knowledge. They contain huge amounts of knowledge in tiny containers. They are able to show the interconnections and the ultimate results.

Learning the Unexpected

Sometimes implementing a KM initiative is a lot less simple than it may initially appear. For instance, simply "outlining" benefits, or illustrating them on a flow-chart, may not convince people to change the way they behave. To adopt new processes. To join the effort.

This was not the only practical lesson the Bank learned along its one-year process of embedding best practice transfer into its core operation. The Bank started out with a few "bad breaks" and "dumb luck."

The bad breaks may sound familiar—they included a middle management that needed a lot of convincing, a downsizing environment, and the usual legacy of fragmented and inefficient IT systems.

These bad breaks were more than offset by four pieces of luck: (1) a dynamic and charismatic leader who was on the lookout for a new strategy; (2) a highly motivated professional staff with (3) a large untapped knowledge potential; and (4) the invention of the Web.

Luck is good, but never sufficient. So to really get things going, the

Bank's KM team designed the following steps: create a compelling business vision of knowledge management; build a robust managerial coalition in support of change; define knowledge management activities in specific monitorable activities; map the knowledge "domains" of the organization; and make the case for an adequate budget.

Finally, they learned from others! Benchmarking best practices in an APQC consortium study helped the Bank learn and leapfrog to being one of the leading practitioners after only a short time.

What did the KM team learn through its experience? A lot, and most of it violated their initial assumptions:

Assumption #1: The assumption that "We know exactly where we are going" was unsound, as the organization kept reinventing itself and finding its way on the knowledge journey.

Assumption #2: "What we need is knowledge." While knowledge is valuable, they also found that there is much valuable know-how that has not yet been authenticated as knowledge. In one sense, says Denning, "Knowledge is yesterday's innovation."

Assumption #3: The idea that an intranet would largely obviate the need for help desks proved illusory. The KM team found that people-to-people contact remained crucial.

Assumption #4: "Systematizing KM will kill it." The KM team hesitated to define KM activities in case it turned it into a supply-driven bureaucracy. Although the danger is still there, Denning reports that in general, describing KM as a system seems to have helped people get comfortable with KM and encourage convergence towards a common institutional vision.

Assumption #5: "A mouse-click away is close enough." This turned out to be wrong. KM has to be embedded in the work process.

The Bank's Scale-up Challenges for the Future

With all the learning it has achieved, the Bank is still facing four key implementation challenges.

Making communities of practice work. Although the communities are organized in a logical fashion, knowledge, being inherently untidy, does not always fall into their logical organization. It sprawls across the boundary lines.

Making the organizational culture shift. It seems like everyone in the Bank is perfectly willing to share. However, Denning has found that the problem with ensuring true flow of knowledge, across the enterprise, is on the demand side, not the supply. People are willing to share—if asked. People simply don't ask.

Getting best practices. The Bank has found that even when you figure out what works, what works some of the time, and what almost never works, a reported best practice invariably leaves out many insights and is hard to keep up-to-date. Developing a dynamic knowledge base remains a major challenge.

Figuring out external access. Since ultimately, the Bank wants to open its knowledge treasure chest to external clients, it must resolve questions of copyright, confidentiality, charging for knowledge, the internal impact of external access, and languages.

SUMMARY: PART FIVE

So what do you do on Monday morning? To summarize, let us be allegorical and cram a year into a fictitious day.

8:30 A.M. Start planning. Assess just where you stand on the KM learning curve. Define your value proposition. You need to know where you are now and where to go before you embark on any change efforts.

9:00 A.M. Find the processes and projects that support your value proposition, find champions to lead your KM quest, inform the rest of the organization, and define a business case strong enough to hold management's attention and commitment.

10:30 A.M. Select a project that gives you a good chance of early success and a testing ground for emerging technologies.

11:00 A.M. Begin your design work by following tried-and-true principles of design, such as employing multidisciplinary teams and addressing process, change management, and business issues for a given project.

12:00 Noon. Break for lunch! (And to get buy-in and understanding in the organization.)

1:30 P.M. Implement, launch your project, train the participants, provide support, observe, learn, and record results to help spread the good word.

4:00 P.M. Organize your learnings from the pilot, and use the lessons to create an expansion strategy that embeds KM and transfer into every area of your organization.

5:00 P.M. Plan the next day—the expansion and scale-up.

Part Six

CONCLUSION

There is no conclusion to managing knowledge and transferring best practices. It is a race without a finishing line. And this is even more true in the knowledge era as we move toward the Millennium.

But there is a conclusion to this book. Before we end, we want to share with you some of the overarching themes of our three large-scale studies on knowledge management and the transfer of best practices. These "consortium" (i.e., multicompany) benchmarkng studies led by APQC included more than seventy of the leading organizations practicing knowledge management in the United States and in Europe.

The organizations in our studies met together frequently, using APQC's benchmarking methodology, and shared their *best practices in knowledge management in their own organizations. Also, they sought out additional "best practices" organizations ("partners") across the United States and Europe, site visited them, and included their knowledge in the findings. These studies are probably the most comprehensive empirical collection of what actually goes on in organizations in knowledge management and the transfer of best practices. (APQC, 1996; APQC, 1997)*

We have already encapsulated some of these findings in the preceding chapters. But in this Conclusion, we share with you ten enduring principles that emerged from the studies, and which will guide you as you move forward.

Chapter 22

ENDURING PRINCIPLES

The APQC's consortium studies on knowledge management and best practice transfer were conducted during 1995–1997 and other studies were under way as this book was published. Participating companies represented a broad range of industries, from computers and electronics to financial/investment and chemicals.

Each of our six-month studies gave us a unique and treasured chance to "peek" behind the scenes of KM at some of the early work, the experimentation, the success stories. Most of our benchmarking participants had been actively involved for years in isolated, fragmented KM efforts. What sets them apart is that they have, more recently, become more conscious and organized in their attempts to manage knowledge and transfer practices. In fact, for some, it wasn't until we approached them about participation in a study that they labeled their growing and successful efforts "knowledge management" or the "transfer of best practices." Our lessons and enduring principles were detailed in final reports (APQC, 1996; APQC,1997).

The following principles will sound familiar because they resonate throughout this book. They are intertwined in the case studies and case examples; they echo the conclusions of many of the book's parts.

Here, in a nutshell, are principles that we believe, for this moment, to hold true.

1. BUSINESS VALUES DRIVE TRANSFER BENEFITS

Where KM and transfer worked, they worked because management aimed efforts at a clear set of value propositions: improving customer-related practices, speeding up product (including service) development, or achieving new levels of operational excellence. The choice depends on the "value levers" in a particular marketplace. For a pharmaceutical firm, quicker product development may be critical, whereas a manufacturing firm may affect performance more by reaching optimal operational efficiency. In all cases, however, stakeholders have bought into the choice of value proposition, and the champion was pursuing it with a vengeance.

2. TRANSFER OF BEST PRACTICES IS THE MOST COMMON, AND MOST EFFECTIVE, KM STRATEGY.

Every partner in our study relied on transfer of internal best practices as a predominant knowledge management strategy. It was not the *only* strategy. But it was the most popular and effective way companies chose to find out and share what they know.

3. KM MUST BE WOVEN INTO THE CORPORATE INFRASTRUCTURE

KM is not a one-person job. To work, it must be part of everyone's agenda, and it must be "institutionalized" through the creation of some specific human and IT support systems. Benchmarking partners typically described KM as a management responsibility, throughout the organization, supported by some shared infrastructure, such as (1) knowledge champions, (2) common technology platforms, and (3) a corporate repository of knowledge, such as a library or database.

4. KM-EARMARKED FUNDING IS RARE

At most KM pioneers, there was little "specific" budget earmarked for KM. Although some resources were centrally dedicated, funding for specific projects and approaches usually resides in the IT department and the business units with a project champion who funds the effort.

5. HAVING THE "RIGHT" CULTURE IS CRITICAL

Every benchmarking partner was convinced that the firm's culture had a strong influence on the effective management of knowledge. Some were fortunate enough to start with a culture supportive of knowledge sharing, such as a strong professional ethic, corporate pride, and well-honed skills in teaming. Those that did not have these cultural attributes listed two prerequisites for building the culture of sharing: *leadership support*, cemented through early successes, and *practice:* The more their companies shared, the better was employee sharing behavior.

6. SUCCESSFUL KM EFFORTS EMPLOY A "PUSH-ME-PULL-YOU" APPROACH

While the debate about push versus pull strategies rages on, we have found that a combination tack seems to work best. Push approaches are characterized by a desire to *capture* knowledge in central repositories, then push it out to the organization. In contrast, pull approaches expect people to *seek* the knowledge they need, when they need it. Neither alone seems to be enough.

7. IF IT WORKS, IT REALLY WORKS

Incentives can't make us act in a counterintuitive manner. The only real way to guarantee sharing is to make sure it is part of everyday work. If you make sure it helps people do their jobs better and faster, they will share! Only a minority of benchmarking partners said they use formal financial rewards to reward sharing behaviors. Mostly, companies choose to embed knowledge development and transfer into their professional and career development systems.

8. TOP-LEVEL SUPPORT IS A MUST

If the KM effort is to survive and succeed, it must enlist the support of top management. There's a clear difference between firms with and firms without such top-level support. Those that have it are going full steam ahead. In one case where top management did not buy into the concept, the effort indeed fizzled and failed. Most of our partners reported one of two ways to "gain" the necessary backup: (1) demonstrate success early on, and (2) present a clear and compelling case for action (the "burning platform").

9. TECHNOLOGY IS A CATALYST BUT NO PANACEA

KM is not about technology, but there is no doubt that the explosive growth and ready adoption of Internet and intranet technologies has indeed been a dramatic catalyst for knowledge sharing. Whereas benchmarking partners were quick to say that IT is only an *enabler* for KM, most admit they would follow a totally different route were IT not around. Indeed, many spend a significant portion of their resources on building a supportive IT architecture.

10. MATURE KM EFFORTS LEAD TO TRANSITION FROM NURTURING TO MEASURING

Measurement was probably the least developed aspect of our partners' work. In fact, several thought too much measurement, too early on, would potentially hinder development. But while early KM efforts have been characterized by experimentation and trial and error, as firms mature, the need to measure success, monitor progress, and design new solutions imposes a new discipline and a quest for more sophisticated yardsticks.

Appendix

The Knowledge Management Assessment Tool (KMAT)©

The KMAT was jointly developed by the American Productivity & Quality Center and Arthur Andersen in 1995 to help organizations self-assess where their strengths and opportunities lie in managing knowledge. For additional information, contact the APQC at: 1-800-776-9676.

The tool is divided into 5 sections: the KM process; leadership; culture; technology; measurement. The following is a subset of the items and information in the KMAT, with a simplified scoring system.

Directions: Read the statements below and evaluate what you think your organization's performance is. The scale is as follows:

1 = no 2 = poor 3 = fair 4 = good 5 = excellent

1. THE KNOWLEDGE MANAGEMENT PROCESS

P1. Knowledge Gaps are systematically identified and well-defined processes are used to close them.

❍ 1 ❍ 2 ❍ 3 ❍ 4 ❍ 5

P2. A sophisticated and ethical intelligence gathering mechanism has been developed.

❍ 1 ❍ 2 ❍ 3 ❍ 4 ❍ 5

P3. All members of the organization are involved in looking for ideas in traditional and *non*traditional places.

❍ 1 ❍ 2 ❍ 3 ❍ 4 ❍ 5

P4. The organization has formalized the process of transferring best practices, including documentation and lessons learned.

❍ 1 ❍ 2 ❍ 3 ❍ 4 ❍ 5

P5. "Tacit" knowledge (what employees know how to do, but cannot express) is valued and transferred across the organization.

❍ 1 ❍ 2 ❍ 3 ❍ 4 ❍ 5

Total of items P1 through P5: ____________

II. LEADERSHIP IN KNOWLEDGE MANAGEMENT

L1. Managing organizational knowledge is central to the organization's strategy.

❍ 1 ❍ 2 ❍ 3 ❍ 4 ❍ 5

L2. The organization understands the revenue-generating potential of its knowledge assets and develops strategies for marketing and selling them.

❍ 1 ❍ 2 ❍ 3 ❍ 4 ❍ 5

L3. The organization uses learning to support existing core competencies and create new ones.

❍ 1 ❍ 2 ❍ 3 ❍ 4 ❍ 5

L4. Individuals are hired, evaluated, and compensated for their contributions to the development of organizational knowledge.

❍ 1 ❍ 2 ❍ 3 ❍ 4 ❍ 5

Total of items L1 through L4: ____________

III. KNOWLEDGE MANAGEMENT CULTURE

C1. The organization encourages and facilitates knowledge sharing.

❍ 1 ❍ 2 ❍ 3 ❍ 4 ❍ 5

C2. A climate of openness and trust permeates the organization.

❍ 1 ❍ 2 ❍ 3 ❍ 4 ❍ 5

C3. Customer value creation is acknowledged as a major objective of knowledge management.

❍ 1 ❍ 2 ❍ 3 ❍ 4 ❍ 5

C4. Flexibility and a desire to innovate drive the learning process.

❍ 1 ❍ 2 ❍ 3 ❍ 4 ❍ 5

C5. Employees take responsibility for their own learning.

❍ 1 ❍ 2 ❍ 3 ❍ 4 ❍ 5

Total of items C1 through C5: ______________

IV. KNOWLEDGE MANAGEMENT TECHNOLOGY

T1. Technology links all members of the enterprise to one another and to all relevant external publics.

❍ 1 ❍ 2 ❍ 3 ❍ 4 ❍ 5

T2. Technology creates an institutional memory that is accessible to the entire enterprise.

❍ 1 ❍ 2 ❍ 3 ❍ 4 ❍ 5

T3. Technology brings the organization closer to its customers.

❍ 1 ❍ 2 ❍ 3 ❍ 4 ❍ 5

T4. The organization fosters development of "human-centered" information technology.

❍ 1 ❍ 2 ❍ 3 ❍ 4 ❍ 5

T5. Technology that supports collaboration is rapidly placed in the hands of employees.

❍ 1 ❍ 2 ❍ 3 ❍ 4 ❍ 5

T6. Information systems are real-time, integrated, and "smart."

❍ 1 ❍ 2 ❍ 3 ❍ 4 ❍ 5

Total of items T1 through T6: ____________

V. KNOWLEDGE MANAGEMENT MEASUREMENT

M1. The organization has invented ways to link knowledge to financial results.

❍ 1 ❍ 2 ❍ 3 ❍ 4 ❍ 5

M2. The organization has developed a specific set of indicators to manage knowledge.

❍ 1 ❍ 2 ❍ 3 ❍ 4 ❍ 5

M3. The organization's set of measures balances hard and soft as well as financial and non-financial indicators.

❍ 1 ❍ 2 ❍ 3 ❍ 4 ❍ 5

M4. The organization allocates resources toward efforts that measurably increase its knowledge base.

❍ 1 ❍ 2 ❍ 3 ❍ 4 ❍ 5

Total of items M1 through M4: ____________

REFERENCES

American Productivity & Quality Center. 1996. *Emerging Best Practices in Knowledge Management*. Houston, Texas.

———. 1997. *Using Information Technology to Support Knowledge Management*. Houston, Texas.

———. 1997. *Strategies for the Learning Organization*. Houston, Texas.

———. 1998. *Expanding Knowledge Management Externally: Putting Your Knowledge to Work for Customers*. Houston, Texas.

Amidon, Debra M., and David Skyrme. July 1997. "Hoffman-La Roche Profits from Knowledge Management." Knowledge Inc., Vol. 2, No. 7, pp. 2–4.

Bell, Daniel, 1973. *The Coming of Post-Industrial Society: A Venture in Social Forecasting*. Basic Books. New York.

Branch, Shelly. October 13, 1997. "What's Eating McDonald's?" *Fortune*, p. 122.

Davenport, Thomas H. November 15, 1997. "The Knowledge Biz." *CIO Magazine*, Vol. 11, No. 4 (Section 2), pp. 32–34.

Davenport, Thomas H., and Lawrence Prusak. 1998. *Working Knowledge*. Harvard Business School Press. Boston.

Drucker, Peter F. 1993. *Post-Capitalist Society*. Butterworth Heinemann. Oxford.

Edvinsson, Leif, and Michael S. Malone. 1997. *Intellectual Capital: Realizing Your Company's True Value by Finding Its Hidden Brainpower*. Harper Business. New York.

Fisher, Anne. October 27, 1997. "Key to Success: People, People, People." *Fortune*. Part of *Fortune*'s annual *The World's Most Admired Companies*.

Hibbard, Justin. October 20, 1997. "Knowing What We Know." *Information Week*. Issue 653. pp. 46–64.

Nonaka, Ikujiro. 1994. "A Dynamic Theory of Organizational Knowledge Creation." *Organizational Science* 5, No. 1, pp. 14–37.

———. 1991. The Knowledge-Creating Company." *Harvard Business Review*, November/December, pp. 96–104.

Nonaka, Ikujiro, and Hirotaka Takeuchi. 1995. *The Knowledge-Creating Company*. Oxford University Press. New York.

Pascarella, Perry. October 1997. "Harnessing Knowledge" *Management Review*, Vol. 86, No. 9, pp. 37–40.

Polyani, Michael. 1958. *Personal Knowledge*. University of Chicago Press. Chicago.

———. 1967. *The Tacit Dimension*. Doubleday. New York.

Stewart, Thomas A. 1997. *Intellectual Capital: The New Wealth of Organizations*. Doubleday. New York.

Svieby, Karl. 1997. *The New Organizational Wealth: Managing and Measuring Knowledge Based Assets*. Berrett-Koehler Publishing. San Francisco.

Szulanski, Gabriel. 1994 *Intra-Firm Transfer of Best Practices Project*. American Productivity and Quality Center. Houston, Texas.

———. 1996. "Exploring Internal Stickiness: Impediments to the Transfer of Best Practice Within the Firm." *Strategic Management Journal*, Vol. 17 (Winter Special Issue), pp. 27–43.

Toffler, Alvin. 1970. *Future Shock*. Random House. New York.

———. 1980. *The Third Wave*. William Morrow. New York.

Treacy, Michael, and Fred Wiersema. 1993. "Customer Intimacy and Other Value Disciplines." *Harvard Business Review*, January/February, pp. 84–93.

———. 1995. *The Discipline of Market Leaders: Choose Your Customers, Narrow Your Focus and Dominate Your Market*. Addison-Wesley Publishing. Reading, Massachusetts.

Van Ewyk, Onno. 1997. Personal communication. HCI Consulting. Sydney, Australia.

INDEX

AA OnLine (Arthur Andersen), 97
Absorptive capacity, lack of, xi, 17
Accountability, 77
Activities, measuring through, 135–36
Africa Region Live Database (LDB) (World Bank), 82, 96, 162
Alliance Revolution (Gomes-Cassares), 142–43
American Airlines, 185
American Productivity & Quality Center (APQC), x, 17, 74, 81, 82, 95, 102, 155, 157, 161, 162, 217, 221, 223, 227
  Consortium Benchmarking Studies, xiii, 12
  Institute for Education Best Practices, x
  International Benchmarking Clearinghouse, x, xi, xiv
Amgen, xiv
Amidon, 57
Amoco Corporation, 37, 76, 77, 115, 119–20, 122
  design phase in, 197–98
  implementation phase in, 205–7
  planning phase in, 189–90
  scale-up phase in, 211–14
AMP, 14–15, 20, 214
Anti-sharing culture, 72
Apple Computer, 128
APQC. *See* American Productivity & Quality Center (APQC)
Aristotle, 3
Arthur Andersen, 9, 23, 37, 42, 61, 83, 90, 97, 115, 136, 157, 192, 227
Asian Benchmarking Center, xiv
AT&T Company, xiv, 113

Baker, Bill, 85
Baker, Jerry, 22
Balanced scorecard (BSC) system, 134–35
Bell, Daniel, 3
Benchmarking, xiv, 34, 184–85, 186, 217, 221, 223
Best practices databases, 95
Best practices
  definition of, 12–13
  transfer of. *See* Knowledge management (KM)
Best Practices KnowledgeBase (Texas Instruments), 92, 97, 112, 121, 155–58
Blackburn, Tom W., 45–46
Blindness, 108
Boeing, 74
British Airways, 74
British Petroleum, 204–5

Buckman Laboratories International, 8, 23, 37, 41, 91, 92, 115, 132, 136, 141, 143, 187, 192, 202, 209, 210
  K'Netix, 117, 133–34, 144–48, 150, 187, 202
  Knowledge Transfer Department (KTD), 103, 116–17, 145, 187
Buckman, Robert, 25, 38, 41, 71, 76, 77, 93, 94, 116, 141, 144, 145, 148–50
Burger King, 49

Callaghan, Michael, 63, 66, 67
Capitalism, 77
Case history system, 145
Chevron, xiv, xv, 6, 8, 9, 13–14, 20, 24, 37, 62–67, 76, 79, 110, 112, 113, 115, 122, 203–4, 214
CIGNA Property & Casualty, 8, 37, 99–102, 134–35, 192
Citibank, xiv, 122
Clarke, Arthur, ix
Coca-Cola, 123, 127
Collaborative relationships, 73, 79, 92–93
Collective sense of purpose, 81–82
Commonwealth Benchmarking Club, xiv
Communities of practice, 96, 115, 200–201, 217
Compaq Computer, 101
Competitive intelligence data, 14
CompuServe, 144, 146, 147
Coopers & Lybrand, 113, 115
Cultural Self-Assessment Test, 72
Culture, as enabler of transfer, 24, 26, 69, 71–84, 224–25
Customer intimacy, 22, 23, 32, 34, 38–46, 67, 68, 133, 171, 187

Data analysis, 95, 100
Databases and datamining tools, 88, 89, 94, 95–96, 101, 112–13, 165
Data-to-knowledge conversion systems, 95, 100, 101
Davenport, Tom, xv, 87, 88
Davis, John, 15
DEC, 170
Decision support, 95
Dell Computers, 34, 35
Demarest, Marc, 41, 50, 78, 171–74, 176
Democracy, 77
Denning, Stephen, 161, 162, 164–65, 169, 215, 217
Derr, Ken, 11, 63–66, 76
Design phase, 26, 181, 182, 191–98, 200
Discipline of Market Leaders, The (Treacy and Wiersema), 22
Discussion databases, 94, 96–97
Domino, 93, 207
Dow Chemical, 8, 37
Drucker, Peter, 3, 38, 142
DuPont, xv

Eastman Kodak, xiv
ECHO (Every Contact Has Opportunity), 44–45
Education Knowledge Management System (EKMS) (World Bank), 79, 162–64, 168
Edvinsson, Leif, 4, 25, 61
Eisenhower, Dwight D., 183
Elsenheimer, Richard, 212
E-mail, 83, 87, 96, 99
Empowerment, 40
Enablers of transfer, xii, 21, 27
  culture, 24, 26, 69, 71–84, 224–25
  infrastructure, 25, 69, 71, 75, 107–25, 224
  measurement, 25, 69, 71, 126–38, 226
  technology, 25, 26, 69, 71, 85–106, 137, 185, 226
Engibous, Tom, 8, 61–62, 153
Ernst & Young, 23, 115–16
European Foundation for Quality Management, xiv, 156

Excalibur, 113
Experts, use of, 66
Explicit knowledge, 3, 19, 21, 88
External benchmarking, xiv, 34, 186

Facilitated transfer, 110–11, 118–22, 125
FedEx, 74
Focus, 31–33, 35, 205
Fortune magazine, 49, 74
Four-phase process, 21, 26, 27
  design phase, 26, 181, 182, 191–98, 200
  implementation phase, 26, 119, 181, 182, 199–207
  planning phase, 26, 181–90, 200
  scale-up phase, 26, 181, 182, 208–19
Frolich, Bruce, 64
Front-end loading, 66

Garvin, David, 10
General Electric, xiv, 35, 74, 77, 123–24
George, Bob, xv
Gleick, James, 127
Gomes-Cassares, Ben, 142–43
GrapeVINE, 113
Greer, Julie, 206
Groupware, 87, 92–93
GTE, xiv

Hay Group, 74
Help-desk technology, 23, 88, 165
Hewlett-Packard, 37, 101, 110, 170
Hidden knowledge, 108
Hiebeler, Bob, 42, 61
Hoffmann-La Roche, 23, 37, 51, 56–58
Home Depot, 34
Hoovers, 113
Huang, Kuan-Tsae, 55, 56
Hughes Space & Communication, 23, 37, 51, 113
Human resource (HR) listings, 98–99
Hypermail, 96, 104, 175

IBM Corporation, xiv, 23, 37, 56, 170, 185
Intellectual Capital Management (ICM) group, 55
Ignorance, as barrier to internal transfer, xi, 17
Implementation phase, 26, 119, 181, 182, 199–207
Individual knowledge, 4
Indonesian Benchmarking Clearinghouse, xiv
Inference, 101
Information technology. *See* Technology, as enabler of transfer
Infrastructure, as enabler of transfer, 25, 69, 71, 75, 107–25, 224
Intellectual capital (IC), 4, 74
Internal benchmarking, xiii, 34, 186
International Benchmarking Clearinghouse (APQC), x, xi, xiv
Internet/intranet technologies, 86, 87, 89–91, 93–94, 104, 159, 226

Johnson, Cindy, 3, 35, 36, 52, 62, 76–77, 80–81, 86, 120, 141, 152–56, 159
Johnson, Samuel, 113
Johnson & Johnson, 35
Junkins, Jerry, ix, 59–60, 120, 152, 153
Junnarkar, Bipin, 53–54, 86, 102

Kaiser Permanente, 8, 37
Kanevsky, Valery, 126
Kanter, Rosabeth Moss, 47
Kerr, Steve, 123–24
KM. *See* Knowledge management (KM)
K'Netix, 117, 133–34, 144–48, 150, 187, 202
Knowledge, definition of, 3–5
Knowledge infrastructure. *See* Infrastructure, as enabler of transfer
Knowledge integrators, 115
Knowledge management (KM)
  barriers to internal transfer, 16–20, 108–9, 111

Knowledge management (*cont.*)
definition of, 5–6
emerging titles, 110, 118
enablers of transfer, 21, 27
culture, 24, 26, 69, 71–84, 224–25
infrastructure, 25, 69, 71, 75, 107–25, 224
measurement, 25, 69, 71, 126–38, 226
technology, 25, 26, 69, 71, 85–106, 137, 185, 226
four-phase process, 21, 26, 27
design phase, 26, 181, 182, 191–98, 200
implementation phase, 26, 119, 181, 182, 199–207
planning phase, 26, 181–90, 200
scale-up phase, 26, 181, 182, 208–19
model for transfer, 21–27
objectives of, 13
value propositions, 21, 27, 29, 31–37, 223–24
customer intimacy, 22, 23, 32, 34, 38–46, 67, 68, 133, 171, 187
definition of, 31
discovering, 186–87
focus and, 31–33, 35
operational excellence, 22, 23–24, 32, 34, 59–68, 133
product-to-market excellence, 22, 23, 32, 34, 47–58, 67, 68, 133
Knowledge Management Assessment Tool (KMAT), 227–30
Knowledge managers, 115
Knowledge services and networks, 110–11, 114–18, 125
KnowledgeSpace, 90
Knowledge Transfer Process, steps in, 4, 6–7
Koskiniemi, Mark, 128, 145, 148, 149, 151
Kraft, 35
Leadership support, 24, 66, 76, 225
LearningSpace, 92
Ledet, Dave, 74, 76, 120, 205–7, 211, 213
Leveraging knowledge as product, 185
Listening, effective, 73
Locator systems, 113, 114
Lost inventions, cost of, 54
Lotus Notes, 86, 87, 89, 92–94, 97, 104, 155–57, 206, 207
Lowrie, William, 76, 77, 190

Magnet content of databases, 96
Malcolm Baldrige Quality Award, 24, 122, 156
Marketing teams, 96
McAdam, John, 117
McDonald's Corporation, 49
McKinsey, 23, 115
Measurement, as enabler of transfer, 25, 69, 71, 126–38, 226
Mergers, 60
Meta Group Inc., The, 94
Michuda, Andy, 98, 114, 124
Microsoft, 74, 127
Miles, Ross, 45
Mission statements, 74
Monsanto, 53–54, 123, 192
Morgan, J.P., 128
Motivation, 17, 80
Motorola, 122
Mutual obligation, 73

National Security Agency (NSA), 7, 12, 37, 115
IDEA (Innovative Development and Enterprise Advancement), 52–53
National Semiconductor, 91, 92, 102–3, 192
NetNews (Sequent), 97
Netscape, 127
Nonaka, Ikujiro, 3, 4, 19
Nurturers, 129–30

O'Brient, Jim, 203
Office space, 79
Operational excellence, 22, 23–24, 32, 34, 59–68, 133
Organizational knowledge, 4
Organizational paralysis, 86
Organizational personalities, 17–20
Organizational structure, layers of, 107–8
Outcomes, measuring through, 131–135
Outsourcing partnerships, 60

Pattilo-Siv, Martha, 79, 163, 164
Pederson, Paul, 50
Peetz, John, 116
PeopleSoft (Sequent), 98
Performance appraisal systems, 24, 83
Performance support systems, 95, 100–101
Personal responsibility, 79–80, 83
Pfizer, 74
Planning phase, 26, 181–90, 200
Plato, 3
Platt, Lew, ix
Pointers to expertise, 95, 97–99, 112, 113
Polanyi, Michael, 3, 19
Preexisting relationships, lack of, xi, 17
Price Waterhouse, 23, 24, 37, 50, 83, 115
Problem resolution systems, 95, 100, 101
Problem-solving paradigms, 73
Process managers, 66
Product-to-market excellence, 22, 23, 32, 34, 47–58, 67, 68, 133
Project work teams, 96
Proof-of-concept, 26
Pro-sharing culture, 72
"Pull" philosophy, 80–81, 225

Quantifiers, 129–30, 137

Real-time intelligent data analysis, 95, 101
Recognition, 83–84
Reengineering paradox, 39–40
Reward and incentive structure, 80, 82–84, 225
Right the First Time program (Hoffman-LaRoche), 57–58
Rosenblum, Judy, 123

Scale-up phase, 26, 181, 182, 208–19
Sears, 185
Section leaders, 25
Self-directed approach to infrastructure design, 110–14, 125
Sequent Computer Systems, Inc., 23, 32–34, 37, 78, 82, 93, 102, 112, 123, 130, 132, 136, 142, 143, 170–79, 187, 192, 210
Sequent Corporate Electronic Library (SCEL), 40–41, 91, 96, 98–99, 117–18, 172–79
Shared Learning, 75–77, 119–20
Shuster, Joseph, 114
Silicon Systems Incorporated, 159
Singapore Quality Award Criteria, 156
Skandia, 8–9, 23, 25, 37, 61, 62
Skyrne, 57
Stock prices, 127–28
Strassmann, Paul, 128
Strategic alliances, 60
Structural knowledge, 4
Structured document repositories, 94, 95–96
Successfully demonstrated practices (SDPs), 15
Sun Microsystems, 127, 170
Superstructure, 108, 122–24
Sveiby, Karl-Erik, 73–74, 86, 193
Swanson, Roger, 74, 142, 170, 172, 178, 179
Szulanski, Gabriel, x–xi, 17, 73, 154

Tacit knowledge, 3–4, 7, 19, 21, 88, 109, 201

Takeuchi, Hirotaka, 19
Team building, 79
Technology, as enabler of transfer, 25, 26, 69, 71, 85–106, 137, 185, 226
Telephone, 87
Teltech Resources Network Corporation, 98, 113, 114, 124
Texas Instruments, xiv, xv, 6, 8, 20, 23–24, 34–37, 52, 61–62, 76–77, 80–81, 83–84, 92, 97, 112, 115, 120–21, 141, 143, 152–59, 192, 209, 210, 214
  Best Practices KnowledgeBase, 92, 97, 112, 121, 155–58
Timmerman, Tim, 45, 46
Toffler, Alvin, 3
Tornberg, Don, 205
Total quality management (TQM), 6, 122
Treacy, Michael, 22, 34, 35

USAA, 9, 23, 37, 43–46, 80
U.S. Postal Service, xiv
"Using Information Technology to Support Knowledge Management" (APQC), 95

Value propositions, 21, 27, 29, 31–37, 223–24
  customer intimacy, 22, 23, 32, 34, 38–46, 67, 68, 133, 171, 187
  definition of, 31
  discovering, 186–87
  focus and, 31–33, 35
  operational excellence, 22, 23–24, 32, 34, 59–68, 133
product-to-market excellence, 22, 23, 32, 34, 47–58, 67, 68, 133
Van Ewyk, Onno, 76, 192–93
Verifone, 8
Video conferencing, 99

Ward, Arian, 51–52
Welch, Jack, 77
Wendy's, 49
Wiersema, Fred, 22, 34, 35
Wolfensohn, James, 142, 160, 214
World Bank, 37, 88, 92, 102, 141–43, 160–69
  Africa Region Live Database (LDB), 82, 96, 162
  Education Knowledge Management System (EKMS), 79, 162–64, 168
  four-phase process in, 214–18

Xerox Corporation, xiv, xv, 20, 185

Year 2000 problem, 89